Apache Kafka 1.0 Cookbook

Over 100 practical recipes on using distributed enterprise messaging to handle real-time data

Raúl Estrada

BIRMINGHAM - MUMBAI

Apache Kafka 1.0 Cookbook

Copyright © 2017 Packt Publishing

All rights reserved. No part of this book may be reproduced, stored in a retrieval system, or transmitted in any form or by any means, without the prior written permission of the publisher, except in the case of brief quotations embedded in critical articles or reviews.

Every effort has been made in the preparation of this book to ensure the accuracy of the information presented. However, the information contained in this book is sold without warranty, either express or implied. Neither the author, nor Packt Publishing, and its dealers and distributors will be held liable for any damages caused or alleged to be caused directly or indirectly by this book.

Packt Publishing has endeavored to provide trademark information about all of the companies and products mentioned in this book by the appropriate use of capitals. However, Packt Publishing cannot guarantee the accuracy of this information.

First published: December 2017

Production reference: 1211217

Published by Packt Publishing Ltd.
Livery Place
35 Livery Street
Birmingham
B3 2PB, UK.

ISBN 978-1-78728-684-9

www.packtpub.com

Credits

Author
Raúl Estrada

Reviewers
Sandeep Khurana
Brian Gatt

Commissioning Editor
Amey Varangaonkar

Acquisition Editor
Varsha Shetty

Content Development Editor
Cheryl Dsa

Technical Editors
Dinesh Pawar

Copy Editor
Safis Editing

Project Coordinator
Nidhi Joshi

Proofreader
Safis Editing

Indexer
Tejal Daruwale Soni

Graphics
Tania Dutta

Production Coordinator
Aparna Bhagat

About the Author

Raúl Estrada has been a programmer since 1996 and a Java developer since 2001. He loves functional languages like Scala, Elixir, Clojure, and Haskell. He also loves all topics related to computer science. With more than 14 years of experience in high availability and enterprise software, he has designed and implemented architectures since 2003. His specialization is in systems integration and he has participated in projects mainly related to the financial sector. He has been an enterprise architect for BEA Systems and Oracle Inc., but he also enjoys mobile programming and game development. He considers himself a programmer before an architect, engineer, or developer.

Raul is a supporter of free software, and enjoys experimenting with new technologies, frameworks, languages, and methods.

> *I want to say thanks to my editors Cheryl Dsa and Dinesh Pawar. Without their effort and patience, it would not have been possible to write this book. I also thank my acquisition editor, Varsha Shetty, who believed in this project from the beginning.*
>
> *And finally, I want to thank all the heroes who contribute (often anonymously and without profit) to open source projects, specifically Apache Kafka. An honorable mention for those who build the connectors of this technology, and especially the Confluent Inc. crew.*

About the Reviewers

Sandeep Khurana is an early proponent in the domain of big data and analytics, which started during his days in Yahoo! (originator of Hadoop). He has been part of many other industry leaders in the same domain such as IBM Software Lab, Oracle, Yahoo!, Nokia, VMware and an array of startups where he was instrumental in architecting, designing and building multiple petabyte scale big data processing systems, which has stood the test of industry rigor. He is completely in his elements with coding in all the big data technologies such as MapReduce, Spark, Pig, Hive, ZooKeeper, Flume, Oozie, HBase, and Kafka. With the wealth of experience arising from being around for 21 years in the industry, he has developed a unique trait of solving the most complicated and critical architectural issues with the simplest and most efficient means. Being an early entrant in the industry he has worked in all aspects of Java/JEE-based technologies and frameworks such as Spring, Hibernate, JPA, EJB, security, and Struts before he delved into the big data domain. Some of his other present areas of interest are OAuth2, OIDC, micro services frameworks, artificial intelligence, and machine learning. He is quite active on LinkedIn (`/skhurana333`) with his tech talks.

Brian Gatt is a software developer who holds a bachelor's degree in computer science and artificial intelligence from the University of Malta, and a masters degree in computer games and entertainment from Goldsmiths University of London. In his spare time, he likes to keep up with the latest in programming, specifically native C++ programming and game development techniques.

www.PacktPub.com

For support files and downloads related to your book, please visit `www.PacktPub.com`. Did you know that Packt offers eBook versions of every book published, with PDF and ePub files available? You can upgrade to the eBook version at `www.PacktPub.com` and as a print book customer, you are entitled to a discount on the eBook copy. Get in touch with us at `service@packtpub.com` for more details. At `www.PacktPub.com`, you can also read a collection of free technical articles, sign up for a range of free newsletters and receive exclusive discounts and offers on Packt books and eBooks.

`https://www.packtpub.com/mapt`

Get the most in-demand software skills with Mapt. Mapt gives you full access to all Packt books and video courses, as well as industry-leading tools to help you plan your personal development and advance your career.

Why subscribe?

- Fully searchable across every book published by Packt
- Copy and paste, print, and bookmark content
- On demand and accessible via a web browser

Customer Feedback

Thanks for purchasing this Packt book. At Packt, quality is at the heart of our editorial process. To help us improve, please leave us an honest review on this book's Amazon page at https://www.amazon.com/dp/1787286843. If you'd like to join our team of regular reviewers, you can email us at customerreviews@packtpub.com. We award our regular reviewers with free eBooks and videos in exchange for their valuable feedback. Help us be relentless in improving our products!

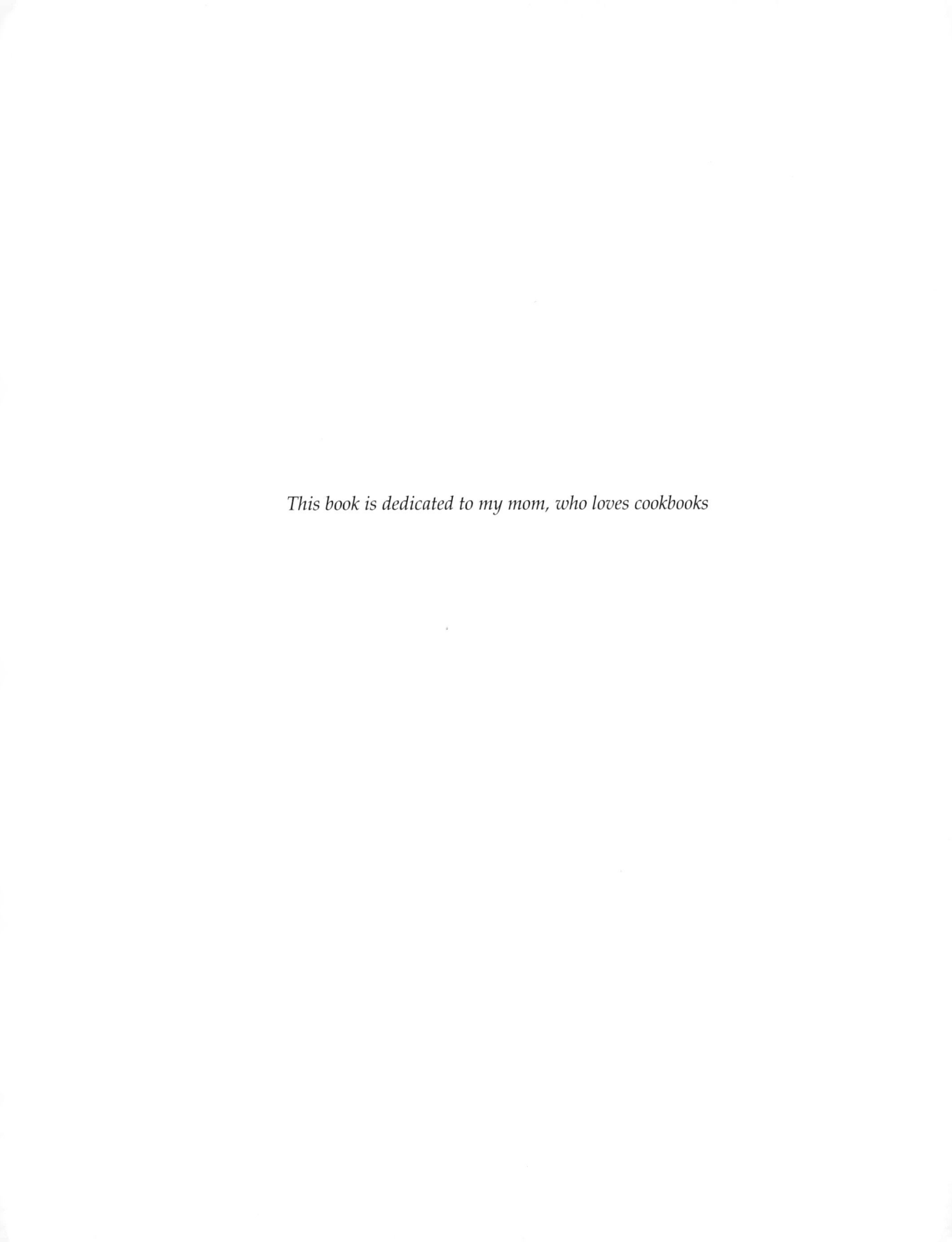

This book is dedicated to my mom, who loves cookbooks

Table of Contents

Preface 1
Chapter 1: Configuring Kafka 9
   Introduction 9
   Installing Kafka 11
      Getting ready 11
      How to do it... 12
          Installing Java in Linux 13
          Installing Scala in Linux 13
          Installing Kafka in Linux 14
      There's more... 14
      See also 17
   Running Kafka 17
      Getting ready 17
      How to do it... 17
      There's more... 18
      See also 18
   Configuring Kafka brokers 18
      Getting ready 19
      How to do it... 19
      How it works... 20
      There's more... 20
      See also 21
   Configuring Kafka topics 21
      Getting ready 22
      How to do it... 22
      How it works... 22
      There's more… 23
   Creating a message console producer 25
      Getting ready 25
      How to do it... 25
      How it works... 25
      There's more… 26
   Creating a message console consumer 27
      Getting ready 27

How to do it... 27
How it works... 27
There's more... 28

Configuring the broker settings 29
Getting ready 29
How to do it... 29
How it works… 29
There's more… 30

Configuring threads and performance 31
Getting ready 31
How to do it... 31
How it works… 31
There's more... 32

Configuring the log settings 32
Getting ready 32
How to do it... 33
How it works… 33
There's more… 34
See also 34

Configuring the replica settings 35
Getting ready 35
How to do it... 35
How it works… 35
There's more... 36

Configuring the ZooKeeper settings 36
Getting ready 36
How to do it… 37
How it works… 37
See also 37

Configuring other miscellaneous parameters 38
Getting ready 38
How to do it... 38
How it works… 39
See also 40

Chapter 2: Kafka Clusters 41
Introduction 41
Configuring a single-node single-broker cluster – SNSB 42
Getting ready 42

How to do it...	43
Starting ZooKeeper	43
Starting the broker	44
How it works...	45
There's more...	45
See also	45
SNSB – creating a topic, producer, and consumer	45
Getting ready	45
How to do it...	46
Creating a topic	46
Starting the producer	47
Starting the consumer	48
How it works...	48
There's more...	48
Configuring a single-node multiple-broker cluster – SNMB	49
Getting ready	49
How to do it...	50
How it works...	51
There's more...	51
See also	51
SNMB – creating a topic, producer, and consumer	51
Getting ready	52
How to do it...	52
Creating a topic	52
Starting a producer	53
Starting a consumer	53
How it works...	53
There's more...	53
See also	54
Configuring a multiple-node multiple-broker cluster – MNMB	54
Getting ready	55
How to do it...	55
How it works...	56
See also	56
Chapter 3: Message Validation	57
Introduction	57
Modeling the events	58
Getting ready	58
How to do it...	58
How it works...	59

There's more...	60
See also	61
Setting up the project	62
Getting ready	62
How to do it...	63
How it works...	65
There's more...	66
See also	66
Reading from Kafka	66
Getting ready	66
How to do it...	67
How it works...	68
There's more...	68
See also	69
Writing to Kafka	69
Getting ready	69
How to do it...	69
How it works...	71
There's more...	71
See also	71
Running ProcessingApp	71
Getting ready	71
How to do it...	72
How it works...	72
There's more...	75
See also	75
Coding the validator	75
Getting ready	76
How to do it...	76
There's more...	78
See also	78
Running the validator	78
Getting ready	78
How to do it...	79
How it works...	79
There's more...	82
See also	82
Chapter 4: Message Enrichment	**83**

Introduction	83
Geolocation extractor	84
Getting ready	84
How to do it...	84
How it works...	87
There's more...	87
See also	87
Geolocation enricher	87
Getting ready	87
How to do it...	88
How it works...	90
There's more...	90
See also	90
Currency price extractor	90
Getting ready	90
How to do it...	91
How it works...	92
There's more...	92
See also	92
Currency price enricher	92
Getting ready	93
How to do it...	94
How it works...	95
There's more...	95
See also	96
Running the currency price enricher	96
Getting ready	96
How to do it...	96
How it works...	97
Modeling the events	99
Getting ready	99
How to do it...	99
How it works...	100
There's more...	101
See also	101
Setting up the project	101
Getting ready	102
How to do it...	102
How it works...	104

There's more...	104
See also	105
Open weather extractor	**105**
Getting ready	105
How to do it...	105
How it works...	106
There's more...	106
See also	107
Location temperature enricher	**107**
Getting ready	107
How to do it...	107
How it works...	109
There's more...	109
See also	109
Running the location temperature enricher	**109**
Getting ready	109
How to do it...	110
How it works...	110
Chapter 5: The Confluent Platform	**113**
Introduction	**113**
Installing the Confluent Platform	**115**
Getting ready	115
How to do it...	116
There's more...	117
See also	117
Using Kafka operations	**117**
Getting ready	117
How to do it...	117
There's more...	120
See also	120
Monitoring with the Confluent Control Center	**120**
Getting ready	120
How to do it...	122
How it works...	124
There's more...	124
Using the Schema Registry	**124**
Getting ready	125
How to do it...	125

See also	129
Using the Kafka REST Proxy	**129**
Getting ready	129
How to do it...	130
There's more...	131
See also	131
Using Kafka Connect	**131**
Getting ready	132
How to do it...	132
There's more...	134
See also	136

Chapter 6: Kafka Streams — 137

Introduction	**137**
Setting up the project	**138**
Getting ready	138
How to do it...	138
How it works...	140
Running the streaming application	**141**
Getting ready	141
How to do it...	141

Chapter 7: Managing Kafka — 145

Introduction	**145**
Managing consumer groups	**145**
Getting ready	146
How to do it...	146
How it works...	147
Dumping log segments	**147**
Getting ready	147
How to do it...	148
How it works...	148
Importing ZooKeeper offsets	**148**
Getting ready	149
How to do it...	149
How it works...	149
Using the GetOffsetShell	**149**
Getting ready	149
How to do it...	150
How it works...	150

Using the JMX tool	150
Getting ready	151
How to do it...	151
How it works...	151
There's more...	152
Using the MirrorMaker tool	152
Getting ready	152
How to do it...	152
How it works...	152
There's more...	153
See also	153
Replaying log producer	153
Getting ready	153
How to do it...	154
How it works...	154
Using state change log merger	154
Getting ready	155
How to do it...	155
How it works...	155
Chapter 8: Operating Kafka	**157**
Introduction	157
Adding or removing topics	157
Getting ready	158
How to do it...	158
How it works...	159
There's more...	160
See also	160
Modifying message topics	160
Getting ready	160
How to do it...	161
How it works...	161
There's more...	162
See also	162
Implementing a graceful shutdown	162
Getting ready	162
How to do it...	163
How it works...	163
Balancing leadership	163

Getting ready	164
How to do it...	164
How it works...	164
There's more...	164
Expanding clusters	**165**
Getting ready	165
How to do it...	165
How it works...	168
There's more...	168
Increasing the replication factor	**169**
Getting ready	169
How to do it...	169
How it works...	169
There's more...	170
Decommissioning brokers	**170**
Getting ready	170
How to do it...	170
How it works...	171
Checking the consumer position	**171**
Getting ready	171
How to do it...	171
How it works...	172

Chapter 9: Monitoring and Security — 173

Introduction	173
Monitoring server statistics	174
Getting ready	174
How to do it...	174
How it works...	177
See also	178
Monitoring producer statistics	178
Getting ready	178
How to do it...	178
How it works...	180
See also	181
Monitoring consumer statistics	181
Getting ready	181
How to do it...	181
How it works...	183

Table of Contents

- See also — 184
- **Connecting with the help of Graphite** — 184
  - Getting ready — 184
  - How to do it... — 184
  - How it works... — 185
  - See also — 186
- **Monitoring with the help of Ganglia** — 186
  - Getting ready — 186
  - How to do it... — 186
  - How it works... — 187
  - See also — 188
- **Implementing authentication using SSL** — 188
  - How to do it... — 188
  - See also — 190
- **Implementing authentication using SASL/Kerberos** — 190
  - How to do it... — 190
  - See also — 191

Chapter 10: Third-Party Tool Integration — 193

- **Introduction** — 193
- **Moving data between Kafka nodes with Flume** — 194
  - Getting ready — 194
  - How to do it... — 194
  - How it works... — 195
  - See also — 196
- **Writing to an HDFS cluster with Gobblin** — 196
  - Getting ready — 197
  - How to do it... — 197
  - How it works... — 198
  - See also — 199
- **Moving data from Kafka to Elastic with Logstash** — 199
  - Getting ready — 200
  - How to do it... — 200
  - How it works... — 200
  - There's more... — 201
  - See also — 201
- **Connecting Spark streams and Kafka** — 201
  - Getting ready — 201
  - How to do it... — 202

How it works...	202
There's more...	203
Ingesting data from Kafka to Storm	203
Getting ready	203
How to do it...	203
How it works...	204
There's more...	204
See also	205
Pushing data from Kafka to Elastic	205
Getting ready	205
How to do it...	205
How it works...	206
See also	206
Inserting data from Kafka to SolrCloud	207
Getting ready	207
How to do it...	207
How it works...	208
See also	208
Building a Kafka producer with Akka	208
Getting ready	209
How to do it...	209
How it works...	210
There's more...	210
Building a Kafka consumer with Akka	210
Getting ready	210
How to do it...	211
Storing data in Cassandra	213
Getting ready	213
How to do it...	213
How it works...	214
Running Kafka on Mesos	214
Getting ready	214
How to do it...	215
How it works...	216
There's more...	217
Reading Kafka with Apache Beam	218
Getting ready	218
How to do it...	218
How it works...	219

There's more...	219
See also	219
Writing to Kafka from Apache Beam	**219**
Getting ready	219
How to do it...	220
How it works...	220
There's more...	220
See also	221
Index	**223**

Preface

Since 2011, Kafka's growth has exploded. More than one-third of all Fortune 500 companies use Apache Kafka. These companies include the top 10 travel companies, 7 of the top 10 banks, 8 of the top 10 insurance companies, and 9 of the top 10 telecom companies.

LinkedIn, Uber, Twitter, Spotify, Paypal, and Netflix process with Apache Kafka, each one with a total of four-comma (1,000,000,000,000) messages in a single day.

Nowadays, Apache Kafka is used for real-time data streaming, to collect data, or to do real-time data analyses. In other contexts, Kafka is used in microservice architectures to improve durability. It can also be used to feed events to **Complex Event Processing** (CEP) architectures and IoT automation systems.

Today we live in the middle of a war, a streaming war. Several competitors (Kafka Streams, Spark Streaming, Akka Streaming, Apache Flink, Apache Storm, Apache Beam, Amazon Kinesis, and so on) are immersed in a competition where there are many factors to evaluate, but mainly the winner is the one with the best performance.

Much of the current adoption of Apache Kafka is due to its ease of use. Kafka is easy to implement, easy to learn, and easy to maintain. Unlike most of its competitors, the learning curve is not so steep.

This book is practical; it is focused on hands-on recipes and it isn't just stop at theoretical or architectural explanations about Apache Kafka. This book is a cookbook, a compendium of practical recipes that are solutions to everyday problems faced in the implementation of a streaming architecture with Apache Kafka. The first part of the book is about programming, and the second part is about Apache Kafka administration.

What this book covers

`Chapter 1`, *Configuring Kafka*, explains the basic recipes used to get started with Apache Kafka. It discusses how to install, configure, and run Kafka. It also discusses how to do basic operations with a Kafka broker.

`Chapter 2`, *Kafka Clusters*, covers how to make three types of clusters: single-node single-broker cluster, single-node multiple-broker cluster, and multiple-node multiple-broker cluster.

Preface

Chapter 3, *Message Validation*, in this chapter having an enterprise service bus, one of the tasks is related to data validation, this is filtering some events from an input message stream. This chapter is about the programming of this validation.

Chapter 4, *Message Enrichment*, details how the next task of an enterprise service bus is related to message enrichment, which means having an individual message, obtaining additional information, and incorporating it into the message stream.

Chapter 5, *The Confluent Platform*, shows how to operate and monitor a Kafka system with the Confluent Platform. It also explains how to use the Schema Registry, the Kafka REST Proxy, and Kafka Connect.

Chapter 6, *Kafka Streams*, explains how to obtain information about a group of messages (a message stream) and additional information such as aggregation and composition of messages using Kafka Streams.

Chapter 7, *Managing Kafka*, talks about the command-line tools developed by the authors of Kafka to make a sysadmin team's life easier when debugging, testing, and running a Kafka cluster.

Chapter 8, *Operating Kafka*, explains the different operations that can be done on a Kafka cluster. These tools cannot be used daily, but they help the DevOps team manage Kafka clusters.

Chapter 9, *Monitoring and Security*, has a first half that talks about various statistics, how they are exposed, and how to monitor them with tools such as Graphite and Ganglia. Its second part is about security—in a nutshell, how to implement SSL authentication, SASL/Kerberos authentication, and SASL/plain authentication.

Chapter 10, *Third-Party Tool Integration*, talks about other real-time data processing tools and how to use Apache Kafka to make a data processing pipeline with them. Tools such as Hadoop, Flume, Gobblin, Elastic, Logstash, Spark, Storm, Solr, Akka, Cassandra, Mesos, and Beam are covered in this chapter.

What you need for this book

The reader should have some experience in programming with Java and some experience in Linux/Unix operating systems.

The minimum configuration needed to execute the recipes in this book is: Intel ® Core i3 processor, 4 GB RAM, and 128 GB of disks. It is recommended to use Linux or Mac OS. Windows is not fully supported.

Who this book is for

This book is for software developers, data architects, and data engineers looking for practical Kafka recipes.

The first half of this cookbook is about programming; this is introductory material for those with no previous knowledge of Apache Kafka. As the book progresses, the difficulty level increases.

The second half of this cookbook is about configuration; this is advanced material for those who want to improve existing Apache Kafka systems or want to better administer current Kafka deployments.

Sections

In this book, you will find several headings that appear frequently (Getting ready, How to do it..., How it works..., There's more..., and See also). To give clear instructions on how to complete a recipe, we use these sections as follows.

Getting ready

This section tells you what to expect in the recipe, and describes how to set up any software or any preliminary settings required for the recipe.

How to do it...

This section contains the steps required to follow the recipe.

How it works...

This section usually consists of a detailed explanation of what happened in the previous section.

There's more...

This section consists of additional information about the recipe in order to make the reader more knowledgeable about the recipe.

See also

This section provides helpful links to other useful information for the recipe.

Conventions

In this book, you will find a number of text styles that distinguish between different kinds of information. Here are some examples of these styles and an explanation of their meaning.

Code words in text, database table names, folder names, filenames, file extensions, pathnames, dummy URLs, user input, and Twitter handles are shown as follows: "Finally, run the `apt-get` update to install the Confluent Platform."

A block of code is set as follows:

```
consumer.interceptor.classes=io.confluent.monitoring.clients.interceptor.MonitoringConsumerInterceptor
producer.interceptor.classes=io.confluent.monitoring.clients.interceptor.MonitoringProducerInterceptor
```

Any command-line input or output is written as follows:

```
> bin/kafka-topics.sh --create --zookeeper localhost:2181 --replication-factor 1 --partitions 1 --topic SNSBTopic
```

New terms and **important words** are shown in bold. Words that you see on the screen, for example, in menus or dialog boxes, appear in the text like this: "From Kafka Connect, click on the **SINKS** button and then on the **New sink** button."

Warnings or important notes appear like this.

Tips and tricks appear like this.

Reader feedback

Feedback from our readers is always welcome. Let us know what you think about this book-what you liked or disliked. Reader feedback is important for us as it helps us develop titles that you will really get the most out of. To send us general feedback, simply e-mail feedback@packtpub.com, and mention the book's title in the subject of your message. If there is a topic that you have expertise in and you are interested in either writing or contributing to a book, see our author guide at www.packtpub.com/authors.

Customer support

Now that you are the proud owner of a Packt book, we have a number of things to help you to get the most from your purchase.

Downloading the example code

You can download the example code files for this book from your account at http://www.packtpub.com. If you purchased this book elsewhere, you can visit http://www.packtpub.com/support and register to have the files e-mailed directly to you. You can download the code files by following these steps:

1. Log in or register to our website using your e-mail address and password.
2. Hover the mouse pointer on the **SUPPORT** tab at the top.
3. Click on **Code Downloads & Errata**.
4. Enter the name of the book in the **Search** box.
5. Select the book for which you're looking to download the code files.
6. Choose from the drop-down menu where you purchased this book from.
7. Click on **Code Download**.

You can also download the code files by clicking on the **Code Files** button on the book's webpage at the Packt Publishing website. This page can be accessed by entering the book's name in the **Search** box. Please note that you need to be logged in to your Packt account. Once the file is downloaded, please make sure that you unzip or extract the folder using the latest version of:

- WinRAR / 7-Zip for Windows
- Zipeg / iZip / UnRarX for Mac
- 7-Zip / PeaZip for Linux

The code bundle for the book is also hosted on GitHub at https://github.com/PacktPublishing/Apache-Kafka-1-Cookbook. We also have other code bundles from our rich catalog of books and videos available at https://github.com/PacktPublishing/. Check them out!

Downloading the color images of this book

We also provide you with a PDF file that has color images of the screenshots/diagrams used in this book. The color images will help you better understand the changes in the output. You can download this file from https://www.packtpub.com/sites/default/files/downloads/ApacheKafka1Cookbook_ColorImages.pdf.

Errata

Although we have taken every care to ensure the accuracy of our content, mistakes do happen. If you find a mistake in one of our books-maybe a mistake in the text or the code-we would be grateful if you could report this to us. By doing so, you can save other readers from frustration and help us improve subsequent versions of this book. If you find any errata, please report them by visiting http://www.packtpub.com/submit-errata, selecting your book, clicking on the **Errata Submission Form** link, and entering the details of your errata. Once your errata are verified, your submission will be accepted and the errata will be uploaded to our website or added to any list of existing errata under the Errata section of that title. To view the previously submitted errata, go to https://www.packtpub.com/books/content/support and enter the name of the book in the search field. The required information will appear under the **Errata** section.

Piracy

Piracy of copyrighted material on the Internet is an ongoing problem across all media. At Packt, we take the protection of our copyright and licenses very seriously. If you come across any illegal copies of our works in any form on the Internet, please provide us with the location address or website name immediately so that we can pursue a remedy. Please contact us at copyright@packtpub.com with a link to the suspected pirated material. We appreciate your help in protecting our authors and our ability to bring you valuable content.

Questions

If you have a problem with any aspect of this book, you can contact us at questions@packtpub.com, and we will do our best to address the problem.

1
Configuring Kafka

In this chapter, we will cover the following topics:

- Installing Kafka
- Running Kafka
- Configuring Kafka brokers
- Configuring Kafka topics
- Creating a message console producer
- Creating a message console consumer
- Configuring the broker settings
- Configuring threads and performance
- Configuring the log settings
- Configuring the replica settings
- Configuring the Zookeeper settings
- Configuring other miscellaneous parameters

Introduction

This chapter explains the basic recipes to get started with Apache Kafka. It discusses how to install, configure, and run Kafka. It also discusses how to make basic operations with a Kafka broker.

Kafka can run in several operating systems: Mac, Linux, and even Windows. As it usually runs in production on Linux servers, the recipes in this book are designed to run in Linux environments. This book also considers the bash environment usage.

Kafka scales very well in a horizontal fashion without compromising speed and efficiency.

This chapter explains how to install, configure, and run Kafka. As this is a practical recipes book, it does not cover the theoretical details of Kafka. These three things are enough theory for the moment:

1. To connect heterogeneous applications, we need to implement a mechanism for message publishing by sending and receiving messages among them. A message router is known as a **message broker**. Kafka is a software solution to deal with routing messages among consumers in a quick way.
2. The message broker has two directives: the first is to not block the producers, and the second is to isolate producers and consumers (the producers should not know who their consumers are).
3. Kafka is two things: a real-time, publish-subscribe solution, and a messaging system. Moreover, it is a solution: open source, distributed, partitioned, replicated, commit-log based, with a publish-subscribe schema.

Before we begin it is relevant to mention some concepts and nomenclature in Kafka:

- **Broker**: A server process
- **Cluster**: A set of brokers
- **Topic**: A queue (that has **log partitions**)
- **Offset**: A message identifier
- **Partition**: An ordered and immutable sequence of records continually appended to a structured commit log
- **Producer**: Those who publish data to topics
- **Consumer**: Those who process the feed
- **ZooKeeper**: The coordinator
- **Retention period**: The time to keep messages available for consumption

In Kafka, there are three types of clusters:

- **Single node**: Single broker
- **Single node**: Multiple Broker
- **Multiple node**: Multiple Broker

There are three ways to deliver messages:

- **Never redelivered**: The messages may be lost
- **May be redelivered**: The messages are never lost
- **Delivered once**: The message is delivered exactly once

There are two types of log compaction:

- **Coarse grained**: By time
- **Finer grained**: By message

The next six recipes contain the necessary steps to make a full Kafka test from zero.

Installing Kafka

This is the first step. This recipe shows how to install Apache Kafka.

Getting ready

Ensure that you have at least 4 GB of RAM in your machine; the installation directory will be `/usr/local/kafka/` for Mac users and `/opt/kafka/` for Linux users. Create these directories.

Configuring Kafka

How to do it...

Go to the Apache Kafka home page at http://kafka.apache.org/downloads, as in *Figure 1-1, Apache Kafka download page*:

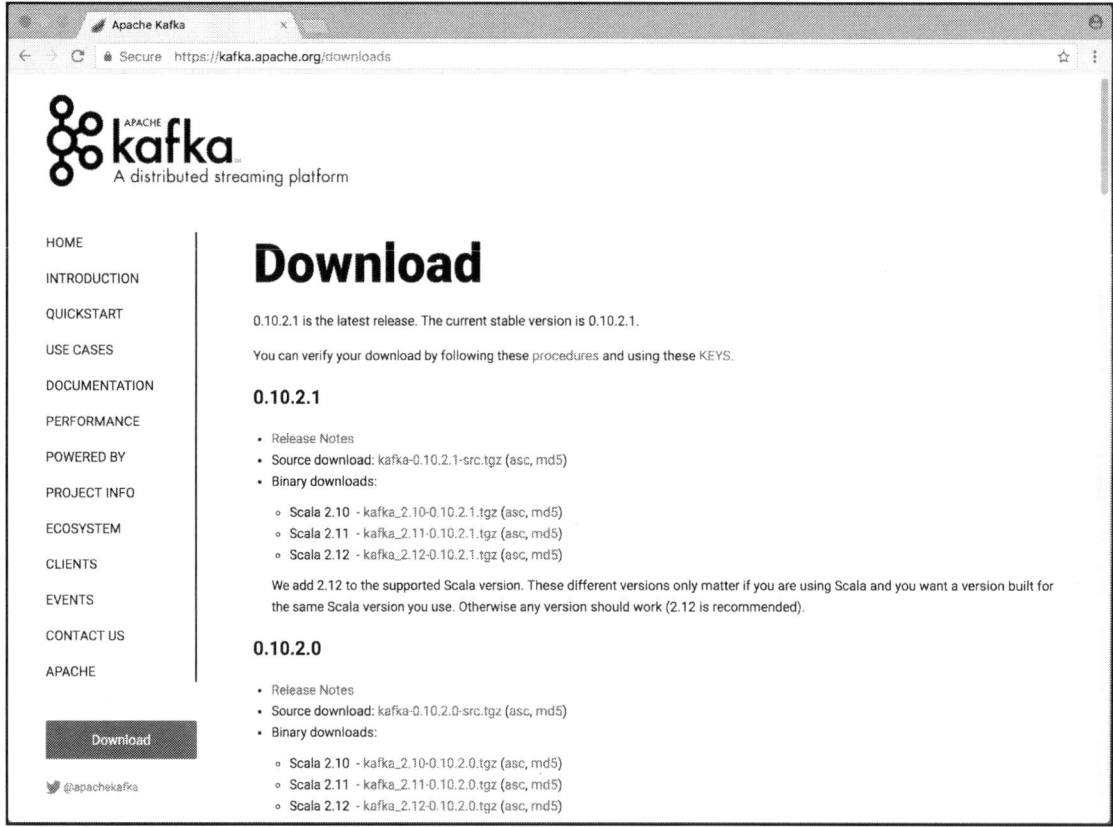

Figure 1-1. Apache Kafka download page

The current available version of Apache Kafka is 0.10.2.1, as a stable release. A major limitation with Kafka since 0.8.x is that it is not backward-compatible. So, we cannot replace this version for one prior to 0.8. Once you've downloaded the latest available release, let's proceed with the installation.

Remember, for Mac users, replace the directory /opt/ for /usr/local/ in the examples.

Installing Java in Linux

We need Java 1.7 or later. Download and install the latest JDK from Oracle's website: http://www.oracle.com/technetwork/java/javase/downloads/index.html

1. Change the file mode:

   > `chmod +x jdk-8u131-linux-x64.rpm`

2. Go to the directory in which you want to perform the installation:

   > `cd <directory path name>`

3. Run the `rpm` installer with the command:

   > `rpm -ivh jdk-8u131-linux-x64.rpm`

4. Finally, add the environment variable `JAVA_HOME`. This command will write the `JAVA_HOME` environment variable to the file `/etc/profile`:

   > `echo "export JAVA_HOME=/usr/java/jdk1.8.0_131" >> /etc/profile`

Installing Scala in Linux

The following are the steps to install Scala in Linux:

1. Download the latest Scala binary from: http://www.scala-lang.org/download
2. Extract the downloaded file `scala-2.12.2.tgz`:

   > `tar xzf scala-2.12.2.tgz`

3. Most tutorials agree that the best place to set environment variables is in the `/etc/profile` file.

4. Create the `SCALA_HOME` environment variable:

   > `export SCALA_HOME=/opt/scala`

5. Add the Scala bin directory to the `PATH` variable:

   > `export PATH=$PATH:$SCALA_HOME/bin`

Installing Kafka in Linux

The following are the steps to install Kafka in Linux:

1. Extract the downloaded file `kafka_2.10-0.10.2.1.tgz`:

    > `tar xzf kafka_2.10-0.10.2.1.tgz`

2. Create the `KAFKA_HOME` environment variable:

    > `export KAFKA_HOME=/opt/kafka_2.10-0.10.2.1`

3. Add the Kafka bin directory to the `PATH` variable:

    > `export PATH=$PATH:$KAFKA_HOME/bin`

Now Java, Scala, and Kafka are installed.

There's more...

To do all these steps in command-line mode, there is a powerful tool for Mac users called **brew** (the equivalent in Linux would be **yum**).

To install from the command line, we use the following steps:

1. With brew, `install sbt` (Scala build tool):

    > `brew install sbt`

    If you already have it (downloaded in the past), upgrade it:

    > `brew upgrade sbt`

    The output is similar to:

    ```
    > brew upgrade sbt
    ==> Upgrading 1 outdated package, with result:
    sbt 0.13.15
    ==> Upgrading sbt
    ==> Using the sandbox
    ==> Downloading
    https://github.com/sbt/sbt/releases/download/v0.13.15/sbt-0.13.15.tgz
    ==> Downloading from
    https://github-cloud.s3.amazonaws.com/releases/279553/09838df4-23c6
    ```

```
-11e7-9276-14
######################################################################
##### 100.0%
==> Caveats
You can use $SBT_OPTS to pass additional JVM options to SBT:
    SBT_OPTS="-XX:+CMSClassUnloadingEnabled -XX:MaxPermSize=256M"
This formula is now using the standard lightbend sbt launcher
script.
Project specific options should be placed in .sbtopts in the root
of your project.
Global settings should be placed in /usr/local/etc/sbtopts
==> Summary
/usr/local/Cellar/sbt/0.13.15: 378 files, 63.3MB, built in 1 minute
5 seconds
```

2. With brew, install Scala:

   ```
   > brew install scala
   ```

   If you already have it (downloaded in the past), upgrade it:

   ```
   > brew upgrade scala
   ```

   The output is similar to:

   ```
   > brew install scala
   ==> Using the sandbox
   ==> Downloading
   https://downloads.lightbend.com/scala/2.12.2/scala-2.12.2.tgz
   ######################################################################
   ##### 100.0%
   ==> Downloading
   https://raw.githubusercontent.com/scala/scala-tool-support/0a217bc/
   bash-completion/sr
   ######################################################################
   ##### 100.0%
   ==> Caveats
   To use with IntelliJ, set the Scala home to:
   /usr/local/opt/scala/idea
   Bash completion has been installed to:
   /usr/local/etc/bash_completion.d
   ==> Summary
   /usr/local/Cellar/scala/2.12.2: 44 files, 19.9MB, built in 19
   seconds
   Mist:Downloads admin1$ scala -version
   Scala code runner version 2.11.8 -- Copyright 2002-2016, LAMP/EPFL
   ```

Configuring Kafka

3. With brew, install Kafka (it also installs **ZooKeeper**):

   ```
   > brew install kafka
   ```

   If you already have it (downloaded in the past), upgrade it:

   ```
   > brew upgrade kafka
   ```

   The output is similar to:

   ```
   > brew install kafka
   ==> Installing dependencies for kafka: zookeeper
   ==> Installing kafka dependency: zookeeper
   ==> Downloading
   https://homebrew.bintray.com/bottles/zookeeper-3.4.9.sierra.bottle.
   tar.gz
   ######################################################################
   ##### 100.0%
   ==> Pouring zookeeper-3.4.9.sierra.bottle.tar.gz
   ==> Using the sandbox
   ==> Caveats
   To have launched start zookeeper now and restart at login:
   brew services start zookeeper
   Or, if you don't want/need a background service you can just run:
   zkServer start
   ==> Summary
   /usr/local/Cellar/zookeeper/3.4.9:
   242 files, 18.2MB
   ==> Installing kafka
   ==> Downloading
   https://homebrew.bintray.com/bottles/kafka-0.10.2.0.sierra.bottle.t
   ar.gz
   ######################################################################
   ##### 100.0%
   ==> Pouring kafka-0.10.2.0.sierra.bottle.tar.gz
   ==> Caveats
   To have launchd start kafka now and restart at login:
   brew services start kafka
   Or, if you don't want/need a background service you can just run:
   zookeeper-server-start /usr/local/etc/kafka/zookeeper.properties &
   kafka-server-start /usr/local/etc/kafka/server.properties
   ==> Summary
   /usr/local/Cellar/kafka/0.10.2.0: 145 files, 37.3MB
   ```

See also

- Take a look at the Apache Kafka download page: http://kafka.apache.org/downloads
- To see more details about brew, visit: https://brew.sh/

Running Kafka

This is the second step. This recipe shows how to test the Apache Kafka installation.

Getting ready

Go to the Kafka installation directory (/usr/local/kafka/ for Mac users and /opt/kafka/ for Linux users):

```
> cd /usr/local/kafka
```

How to do it...

1. First of all, we need to run Zookeeper (sorry, the Kafka dependency on Zookeeper is still very strong):

    ```
    zkServer start
    ```

    You will get the following result:

    ```
    ZooKeeper JMX enabled by default
    Using config: /usr/local/etc/zookeeper/zoo.cfg
    Starting zookeeper ... STARTED
    ```

2. To check if Zookeeper is running, use the lsof command over the port 9093 (default port):

    ```
    > lsof -i :9093
    ```

You will get the following output:

```
COMMAND    PID    USER    FD    TYPE              DEVICE SIZE/OFF NODE
NAME
java     17479  admin1   97u   IPv6 0xcfbcde96aa59c3bf     0t0 TCP
*:9093 (LISTEN)
```

3. Now run the Kafka server that comes with the installation; go to `/usr/local/kafka/` for Mac users and `/opt/kafka/` for Linux users, as follows:

```
> ./bin/kafka-server-start.sh /config/server.properties
```

Now there is an Apache Kafka broker running on your machine.

There's more...

Remember that Zookeeper must be running on the machine before you start Kafka. If you don't want to start Zookeeper every time you need to run Kafka, install it as an operating system autostart service.

See also

- To experiment in making the Apache Kafka quick start, follow the instructions at https://kafka.apache.org/quickstart

Configuring Kafka brokers

This recipe shows how to deal with the Kafka brokers' basic configuration. For learning and development purposes, one can run Kafka in standalone mode. The real Kafka power is unlocked when it is running with replication in cluster mode and the topics are partitioned accordingly.

There are two main advantages of the cluster mode: parallelism and redundancy. **Parallelism** is the capacity to run tasks simultaneously among the cluster members. **Redundancy** warrants that when a Kafka node goes down, the cluster is safe and accessible from the other nodes.

Single node clusters are not recommended for production environments, so this recipe shows how to configure a cluster with several nodes.

Getting ready

Go to the Kafka installation directory (`/usr/local/kafka/` for Mac users and `/opt/kafka/` for Linux users):

```
> cd /usr/local/kafka
```

How to do it...

As already said, a broker is a server's instance. This recipe shows how to start two different servers on one machine. There is a server configuration template called `server.properties` located in the Kafka installation directory in the `config` sub-directory:

1. For each Kafka broker (server) that we want to run, we make a copy of the configuration file template and rename it accordingly. In this example, the cluster is called `synergy`:

   ```
   > cp config/server.properties synergy-1.properties
   > cp config/server.properties synergy-2.properties
   ```

2. Modify each file according to the plan. If the file is called `synergy-1`, the `broker.id` should be 1. Specify the `port` in which the server should run; the recommendation is 9093 for `synergy-1` and 9094 for `synergy-2`. The `port` property is not set in the template, so add the line accordingly. Finally, specify the location of the Kafka logs (specific archives to store all the Kafka broker operations); in this case, we use the directory `/tmp`.

   In `synergy-1.properties`, set:
   ```
   broker.id=1
   port=9093
   log.dir=/tmp/synergy-1-logs
   ```

In `synergy-2.properties`, set:
```
broker.id=2
port=9094
log.dir=/tmp/synergy-2-logs
```

3. Start the Kafka brokers using the `kafka-server-start.sh` command with the corresponding configuration file. Don't forget that Zookeeper must be already running with its corresponding Kafka node and the ports should not be in use by another process:

```
> bin/kafka-server-start.sh synergy-1.properties &
...
> bin/kafka-server-start.sh synergy-2.properties &
```

Recall that trailing `&` is to specify that you want your command line back. If you want to see the broker output, it is recommended that you run each command in its own command-line window.

How it works...

The properties file contains the server configuration. The `server.properties` file located in the `config` directory is just a template.

All of the members of the cluster should point to the same Zookeeper cluster. Every broker is identified inside the cluster by the name specified in the `broker.id` property. If the `port` property is not specified, Zookeeper will assign the same port number and will overwrite the data. If `log.dir` is not specified, all the brokers will write to the same default `log.dir`. If the brokers are going to run on different machines, then `port` and `log.dir` might not be specified.

There's more...

Before assigning a port to a server, there is a useful command to see what process is running on a specific port (in this case, the port `9093`):

```
> lsof -i :9093
```

The output of the previous command is something like this:

```
COMMAND    PID   USER   FD   TYPE             DEVICE SIZE/OFF NODE NAME
java     17479  admin   97u  IPv6 0xcfbcde96aa59c3bf     0t0  TCP *:9093
(LISTEN)
```

Try to run this command before starting the Kafka servers and run it after starting to see the change. Also, try to start a broker on a port in use to see how it fails.

To run Kafka nodes on different machines, change the ZooKeeper connection string in the configuration file; its default value is:

```
zookeeper.connect=localhost:2181
```

This value is correct only if you are running the Kafka broker on the same machine as Zookeeper. In production, it could not happen. To specify that ZooKeeper is running on different machines (that is, in a ZooKeeper cluster), set:

```
zookeeper.connect=localhost:2181, 192.168.0.2:2183, 192.168.0.3:2182
```

The previous line says that Zookeeper is running on the localhost machine on port `2181`, on the machine with IP Address `192.168.0.2` on port `2183`, and on the machine with IP Address `192.168.0.3` on port `2182`. The Zookeeper default port is `2181`, so try to run it there.

As an exercise, try to raise a broker with incorrect information about Zookeeper. Also, in combination with the `lsof` command, try to raise Zookeeper on a port in use.

See also

- The `server.properties` template (as all the Kafka projects) is published online at: https://github.com/apache/kafka/blob/trunk/config/server.properties

Configuring Kafka topics

The Kafka cluster is running, but the magic inside a broker is the queues, that is, the topics. This recipe shows the second step: how to create Kafka topics.

Getting ready

At this point, you need to:

- Have installed Kafka
- Have Zookeeper up and running
- Have a Kafka server up and running
- Go to the Kafka installation directory (`/usr/local/kafka/` for Mac users and `/opt/kafka/` for Linux users):

    ```
    cd /usr/local/kafka
    ```

How to do it...

Recall that almost all modern projects have two ways to do things: through the command line and through code. Yes, believe or not, the Kafka brokers' creation can be done through code in almost all the modern programming languages; the previous recipe showed just the command-line method. In later chapters, the process to achieve it programmatically is explained.

The same goes for the topics. They can be created through the command line and through code. In this recipe, we will show it through the command line. Kafka has built-in utilities to create brokers (as already shown) and topics. From the Kafka installation directory, type the following command:

```
> ./bin/kafka-topics.sh --create --zookeeper localhost:2181 --replication-factor 1 --partitions 1 --topic humbleTopic
```

The output should be:

```
Created topic "humbleTopic".
```

How it works...

Here, the `kafka-topics.sh` command is used. With the `--create` parameter, it is specified that we want to create a new topic. The `--topic` parameter set the name of the topic; in this case, `humbleTopic`.

The `--replication-factor` parameter is very important; it specifies how many servers of the cluster the topic is going to be replicated in (we mean, running). One broker can run just one replica. Obviously, if we specify a number greater than the number of running servers on the cluster, it is an error (don't be shy and try it in your environment), like this:

```
Error while executing topic command : replication factor: 3 larger than
available brokers: 1
[2017-02-28 07:13:31,350] ERROR
org.apache.kafka.common.errors.InvalidReplicationFactorException:
replication factor: 3 larger than available brokers: 1
   (kafka.admin.TopicCommand$)
```

The `--partitions` parameter, as its name implies, says how many partitions our topic will have. The number of partitions determines the parallelism that can be achieved on the consumer's side. This parameter is fundamental when doing fine tuning on the cluster.

Finally, the `--zoookeeper` parameter indicates where the Zookeeper cluster is running.

When a topic is created, the output in the broker log is something like this:

```
[2017-02-28 07:05:53,910] INFO [ReplicaFetcherManager on broker 1] Removed
fetcher for partitions humbleTopic-0 (kafka.server.ReplicaFetcherManager)
[2017-02-28 07:05:53,950] INFO Completed load of log humbleTopic-0 with 1
log segments and log end offset 0 in 21 ms (kafka.log.Log)
```

This message says that a new topic has been born in that broker.

There's more...

Yes, there are more parameters than `--create`. To check whether a topic has been successfully created, run the `kafka-topics` command with the `--list` parameter:

```
> ./bin/kafka-topics.sh --list --ZooKeeper localhost:2181 humbleTopic
```

This parameter returns the list of all the existent topics in the Kafka cluster.

To get the details of a particular topic, run the `kafka-topics` command with the `--describe` parameter:

```
> ./bin/kafka-topics.sh --describe --zookeeper localhost:2181 --topic
humbleTopic
```

Configuring Kafka

The command output is:

```
Topic:humbleTopic    PartitionCount:1    ReplicationFactor:1    Configs:
Topic: humbleTopic    Partition: 0   Leader: 1    Replicas: 1    Isr: 1
```

The explanation of the output is:

- `PartitionCount`: Number of partitions existing on this topic.
- `ReplicationFactor`: Number of replicas existing on this topic.
- `Leader`: Node responsible for the reading and writing operations of a given partition.
- `Replicas`: List of brokers replicating the Kafka data. Some of these might even be dead.
- `ISR`: List of nodes that are currently in-sync replicas.

To create a topic with multiple replicas, we need to increase the replication factor as follows:

```
> ./bin/kafka-topics.sh --create --zookeeper localhost:2181 --replication-factor 2 --partitions 1 --topic replicatedTopic
```

The output is as follows:

```
Created topic "replicatedTopic".
```

Call the `kafka-topics` command with the `--describe` parameter to check the topic details:

```
> ./bin/kafka-topics.sh --describe --zookeeper localhost:2181 --topic replicatedTopic
Topic:replicatedTopic PartitionCount:1    ReplicationFactor:2    Configs:
Topic: replicatedTopic    Partition: 0   Leader: 1    Replicas: 1,2 Isr: 1,2
```

As Replicas and **ISR (in-sync replicas)** are the same lists, all the nodes are in-sync.

Try to play with all these commands; try to create replicated topics on dead servers and see the output. Also, create topics on running servers and then kill them to see the results.

As mentioned before, all the commands executed through the command line can be executed programmatically.

[24]

Creating a message console producer

Kafka also has a command to produce data through the console. The input can be a text file or the console standard input. Each line typed in the input is sent as a single message to the Kafka cluster.

Getting ready

For this recipe, you need the execution of the previous recipes in this chapter: Kafka already downloaded and installed, the Kafka nodes up and running, and a topic created inside the cluster. To begin producing some messages from the console, change to the Kafka directory in the command line.

How to do it...

Go to the Kafka installation directory (`/usr/local/kafka/` for Mac users and `/opt/kafka/` for Linux users):

```
> cd /usr/local/kafka
```

Run this command, followed by the lines to be sent as messages to the server:

```
./bin/kafka-console-producer.sh --broker-list localhost:9093 --topic humbleTopic

Her first word was Mom

Her second word was Dad
```

How it works...

The previous command pushes two messages to the `humbleTopic` running on the localhost machine on the port 9093.

This is a simple way to check if a broker with a specific topic is up and running as expected.

There's more...

The `kafka-console-producer` program receives the following parameters:

- `--broker-list`: Specifies the Zookeeper servers, specified as a comma-separated list of hostname and ports.
- `--topic`: Followed by the target topic's name.
- `--sync`: This parameter specifies whether the messages should be sent synchronously.
- `--compression-codec`: This parameter specifies the compression codec used to produce the messages. The possible options are: `none`, `gzip`, `snappy`, or `lz4`. If not specified, the default is `gzip`.
- `--batch-size`: The number of messages sent in a single batch if they are not sent synchronously. The batch's size value is specified in bytes.
- `--message-send-max-retries`: Communication is not perfect; the brokers can fail receiving messages. This parameter specifies the number of retries before a producer gives up and drops the message. The number following this parameter must be a positive integer.
- `--retry-backoff-ms`: The election of leader nodes might take some time. This is the time to wait before the producer retries after this election. The number following this parameter is the time in milliseconds.
- `--timeout`: If set and the producer is running in asynchronous mode, this gives the maximum amount of time a message will queue awaiting sufficient batch size. The value is given in milliseconds.
- `--queue-size`: If set and the producer is running in asynchronous mode, this gives the maximum amount of time messages will queue awaiting sufficient batch size.

When doing server fine tuning, the `batch-size`, `message-send-max-retries`, and `retry-backoff-ms` are fundamental; take these parameters into consideration to achieve the desired performance.

Just a moment; someone could say, *Eeey, I don't want to waste my precious time typing all the messages.* For those people, the command receives a file where each line is considered a message:

```
> ./bin/kafka-console-producer.sh --broker-list localhost:9093 --topic humbleTopic < firstWords.txt
```

If you want to see the complete list of arguments, take a look at the command source code at: `https://apache.googlesource.com/kafka/+/0.8.2/core/src/main/scala/kafka/tools/ConsoleProducer.scala`

Creating a message console consumer

Now, take the last step. In the previous recipes, it was explained how to produce messages from the console; this recipe indicates how to read the messages generated. Kafka also has a fancy command-line utility that enables consuming messages. Recall that all the command-line tasks can also be done programmatically. Also, recall that each line of the input was considered a message from the producer.

Getting ready

For this recipe, the execution of the previous recipes in this chapter is needed: Kafka already downloaded and installed, the Kafka nodes up and running, and a topic created inside the cluster. Also, some messages need to be produced with the message console producer. To begin consuming some messages from the console, change to the Kafka directory in the command line.

How to do it...

Consuming messages through the console is easy; just run the following command:

```
> ./bin/kafka-console-consumer.sh --topic humbleTopic --bootstrap-server localhost:9093 --from-beginning

Her first word was Mom
Her second word was Dad
```

How it works...

The parameters are the topic and broker names of the producer. Also, the `--from-begining` parameter specifies that messages should be consumed from the beginning instead of the last messages in the log (go and give it a try: generate many more messages and don't specify this parameter).

Configuring Kafka

There's more...

There are more useful parameters for this command; some interesting ones are:

- `--fetch-size`: The amount of data to be fetched in a single request. The size in bytes follows this argument. The default value is 1024 * 1024.
- `--socket-buffer-size`: The size of the `TCP RECV`. The size in bytes follows this argument. The default value is 2 * 1024 * 1024.
- `--formater`: The name of a class to use for formatting messages for display. The default value is `NewlineMessageFormatter` (already presented in the recipe).
- `--autocommit.interval.ms`: The time interval at which to save the current offset (the offset concept will be explained later) in milliseconds. The time in milliseconds follows the argument. The default value is 10,000.
- `--max-messages`: The maximum number of messages to consume before exiting. If not set, the consumption is continual. The number of messages follows the argument.
- `--skip-message-on-error`: If there is an error while processing a message, the system should skip it instead of halt.

Enough boring theory; this is a practical cookbook, so look at these most solicited menu entries:

Consume just one message:

```
> ./bin/kafka-console-consumer.sh --topic humbleTopic --bootstrap-server localhost:9093 --max-messages 1
```

Consume one message from an offset:

```
> ./bin/kafka-console-consumer.sh --topic humbleTopic --bootstrap-server localhost:9093 --max-messages 1 --formatter 'kafka.coordinator.GroupMetadataManager$OffsetsMessageFormatter'
```

Consume messages from a specific consumer group (consumer groups will be explained further):

```
> ./bin/kafka-console-consumer.sh --topic humbleTopic --bootstrap-server localhost:9093 --new-consumer --consumer-property group.id=my-group
```

If you want to see the complete list of arguments, take a look at the command source code at: https://github.com/kafka-dev/kafka/blob/master/core/src/main/scala/kafka/consumer/ConsoleConsumer.scala

Configuring the broker settings

Most of Apache Kafka's magic is achieved through configuration. As with all the intensive messaging systems, the success factor is to configure them well. In this point, Kafka is highly configurable. In practice, most of the systems have average performance with the default settings, but in production, it is required to configure it to achieve optimal performance. Sometimes, finding the right configuration is a test and error task; there is no such thing as a configuration silver bullet.

The rest of the chapter is about Kafka broker fine tuning.

Getting ready

In previous recipes, it was explained how to install and run Kafka. Now, make a copy of the `server.properties` template in the `config` directory and open the copy with a text editor.

How to do it...

1. Configure the basic settings in the configuration file.
2. Set each one of the following parameters with these values:

   ```
   broker.id=0
   listeners=PLAINTEXT://localhost:9093
   log.dirs=/tmp/kafka-logs
   ```

How it works...

As shown in the previous recipes, all of the broker definition is contained in the configuration file. The rest is to pass the configuration file as an argument to the `server-start` command.

A detailed explanation of every parameter is as follows:

- `broker.id`: A non-negative integer; the default value is 0. The name should be unique in the cluster. The important point here is to assign a name to the broker, so when it is moved to a different host or to a different port, no change is made in the consumer's side.
- `listeners`: A comma-separated list of URIs the broker will listen on and the listener names. Examples of legal listener lists are: `PLAINTEXT://127.0.0.1:9092`, `SSL://:9091`, `CLIENT://0.0.0.0:9092`, and `REPLICATION://localhost:9093`.
- `host.name`: DEPRECATED. A string; the default value is null. If it is not specified, Kafka will bind all the interfaces on the system. If it is specified, it will bind only to the specified address. Set this name if you want the clients to connect to a particular interface.
- `port`: DEPRECATED. A non-negative integer; the default value is `9092`. It is the TCP port in which listen connections. Note that in the file template this value is not set.
- `log.dir`: A String; the default value is `/tmp/kafka-logs`. This is the directory where Kafka persists the messages locally. This parameter tells the directory where Kafka will store the data. It is very important that the user that runs the start command have write permissions on that directory.
- `log.dirs`: A String; the default value is null. This is the directory where Kafka persists the messages locally. If not set, the value in `log.dir` is used. There can be more than one location specified, separating the directories with a comma.

There's more...

If bridged connections are used, it means that when the internal `host.name` and `port` are different from the ones which external parties need to connect to, this parameter is used:

- `advertised.listeners`: The hostname given to producers, consumers, and other brokers specified to connect to. If it is not specified, it is the same as `host.name`.

Configuring threads and performance

No parameter should be left by default when the optimal performance is desired. These parameters should be taken into consideration to achieve the best behavior.

Getting ready

With your favorite text editor, open your `server.properties` file copy.

How to do it...

Adjust the following parameters:

```
message.max.bytes=1000000
num.network.threads=3
num.io.threads=8
background.threads=10
queued.max.requests=500
socket.send.buffer.bytes=102400
socket.receive.buffer.bytes=102400
socket.request.max.bytes=104857600
num.partitions=1
```

How it works...

With these changes, the network and performance configurations have been set to achieve optimum levels for the application. Again, every system is different, and you might need to experiment a little to come up with the optimal one for a specific configuration.

Here is an explanation of every parameter:

- `message.max.bytes`: Default value: 10 00 000. This is the maximum size, in bytes, for each message. This is designed to prevent any producer from sending extra large messages and saturating the consumers.
- `num.network.threads`: Default value: 3. This is the number of simultaneous threads running to handle a network's request. If the system has too many simultaneous requests, consider increasing this value.

- `num.io.threads`: Default value: 8. This is the number of threads for Input Output operations. This value should be at least the number of present processors.
- `background.threads`: Default value: 10. This is the number of threads for background jobs. For example, old log files deletion.
- `queued.max.requests`: Default value: 500. This is the number of messages queued while the other messages are processed by the I/O threads. Remember, when the queue is full, the network threads will not accept more requests. If your application has erratic loads, set this to a value at which it will not throttle.
- `socket.send.buffer.bytes`: Default value: 102 400. This is `SO_SNDBUFF` buffer size, used for socket connections.
- `socket.receive.buffer.bytes`: Default value: 102 400. This is `SO_RCVBUFF` buffer size, also used for socket connections.
- `socket.request.max.bytes`: Default value: 104 857 600. This is the maximum request size, in bytes, that the server can accept. It should always be smaller than the Java heap size.
- `num.partitions`: Default value: 1. This is the number of default partitions of a topic, without giving any partition size.

There's more...

As with everything that runs on the JVM, the Java installation should be tuned to achieve optimal performance. This includes the settings for heap, socket size, memory parameters, and garbage collection.

Configuring the log settings

Log refers to the file where all the messages are stored in the machine; here (in this book), when log is mentioned, think in terms of data structures, not just event recording.

The log settings are fundamental, so it is the way the messages are persisted in the broker machine.

Getting ready

With your favorite text editor, open your `server.properties` file copy.

How to do it...

Adjust the following parameters:

```
log.segment.bytes=1073741824
log.roll.hours=168
log.cleanup.policy=delete
log.retention.hours=168
log.retention.bytes=-1
log.retention.check.interval.ms= 30000
log.cleaner.enable=false
log.cleaner.threads=1
log.cleaner.backoff.ms=15000
log.index.size.max.bytes=10485760
log.index.interval.bytes=4096
log.flush.interval.messages=Long.MaxValue
log.flush.interval.ms=Long.MaxValue
```

How it works...

Here is an explanation of every parameter:

- `log.segment.bytes`: Default value: 1 GB. This defines the maximum segment size in bytes (the concept of segment will be explained later). Once a segment file reaches that size, a new segment file is created. Topics are stored as a bunch of segment files in the log directory. This property can also be set per topic.
- `log.roll.{ms,hours}`: Default value: 7 days. This defines the time period after a new segment file is created, even if it has not reached the size limit. This property can also be set per topic.
- `log.cleanup.policy`: Default value: delete. Possible options are delete or compact. If the delete option is set, the log segments will be deleted periodically when it reaches its time threshold or size limit. If the compact option is set, log compaction is used to clean up obsolete records. This property can also be set per topic.
- `log.retention.{ms,minutes,hours}`: Default value: 7 days. This defines the time to retain the log segments. This property can also be set per topic.
- `log.retention.bytes`: Default value: -1. This defines the number of logs per partition to retain before deletion. This property can also be set per topic. The segments are deleted when the log time or size limits are reached.

- `log.retention.check.interval.ms`: Default value is five minutes. This defines the time periodicity at which the logs are checked for deletion to meet retention policies.
- `log.cleaner.enable`: To enable log compaction, set this to true.
- `log.cleaner.threads`: Indicates the number of threads working on clean logs for compaction.
- `log.cleaner.backoff.ms`: Periodicity at which the logs will check whether any log needs cleaning.
- `log.index.size.max.bytes`: Default value: 1 GB. This sets the maximum size, in bytes, of the offset index. This property can also be set per topic.
- `log.index.interval.bytes`: Default value: 4096. The interval at which a new entry is added to the offset index (the offset concept will be explained later). In each fetch request, the broker does a linear scan for this number of bytes to find the correct position in the log to begin and end the fetch. Setting this value too high may mean larger index files and more memory used, but less scanning.
- `log.flush.interval.messages`: Default value: 9 223 372 036 854 775 807. The number of messages kept in memory before flushed to disk. It does not guarantee durability, but gives finer control.
- `log.flush.interval.ms`: Sets maximum time in ms that a message in any topic is kept in memory before it is flushed to disk. If not set, it is used the value in `log.flush.scheduler.interval.ms`.

There's more...

All of the settings are listed at: `http://kafka.apache.org/documentation.html#brokerconfigs`.

See also

- More information about log compaction is available here: `http://kafka.apache.org/documentation.html#compaction`

Configuring the replica settings

The replication is configured for reliability purposes. Replication can also be tuned.

Getting ready

With your favorite text editor, open your `server.properties` file copy.

How to do it...

Adjust the following parameters:

```
default.replication.factor=1
replica.lag.time.max.ms=10000
replica.fetch.max.bytes=1048576
replica.fetch.wait.max.ms=500
num.replica.fetchers=1
replica.high.watermark.checkpoint.interval.ms=5000
fetch.purgatory.purge.interval.requests=1000
producer.purgatory.purge.interval.requests=1000
replica.socket.timeout.ms=30000
replica.socket.receive.buffer.bytes=65536
```

How it works...

Here is an explanation of these settings:

- `default.replication.factor`: Default value: 1. For an automatically created topic, this sets how many replicas it has.
- `replica.lag.time.max.ms`: Default value: 10 000. There are leaders and followers; if a follower has not sent any fetch request or is not consumed up in at least this time, the leader will remove the follower from the ISR list and consider the follower dead.
- `replica.fetch.max.bytes`: Default value: 1 048 576. In each request, for each partition, this value sets the maximum number of bytes fetched by a request from its leader. Remember that the maximum message size accepted by the broker is defined by `message.max.bytes` (broker configuration) or `max.message.bytes` (topic configuration).

- `replica.fetch.wait.max.ms`: Default value: 500. This is the maximum amount of time for the leader to respond to a replica's fetch request. Remember that this value should always be smaller than the `replica.lag.time.max.ms`.
- `num.replica.fetchers`: Default value: 1. The number of fetcher threads used to replicate messages from a source broker. Increasing this number increases the I/O rate in the following broker.
- `replica.high.watermark.checkpoint.interval.ms`: Default value: 500. The **high watermark** (**HW**) is the offset of the last committed message. This value is the frequency at which each replica saves its high watermark to the disk for recovery.
- `fetch.purgatory.purge.interval.requests`: Default value: 1000. Purgatory is the place where the fetch requests are kept on hold till they can be serviced (great name, isn't?). The purge interval is specified in number of requests (not in time) of the fetch request purgatory.
- `producer.purgatory.purge.interval.requests`: Default value: 1000. It sets the purge interval in number of requests (not in time) of the producer request purgatory (do you catch the difference to the previous parameter?).

There's more...

Some other settings are listed here: `http://kafka.apache.org/documentation.html#brokerconfigs`

Configuring the ZooKeeper settings

Apache Zookeeper is a centralized service for maintaining configuration information providing distributed synchronization. ZooKeeper is used in Kafka for cluster management and to maintain the topics information synchronized.

Getting ready

With your favorite text editor, open your `server.properties` file copy.

How to do it...

Adjust the following parameters:

```
zookeeper.connect=127.0.0.1:2181,192.168.0.32:2181
zookeeper.session.timeout.ms=6000
zookeeper.connection.timeout.ms=6000
zookeeper.sync.time.ms=2000
```

How it works...

Here is an explanation of these settings:

- `zookeeper.connect`: Default value: null. This is a comma-separated value in the form of the `hostname:port` string, indicating the Zookeeper connection. Specifying several connections ensures the Kafka cluster reliability and continuity. When one node fails, Zookeeper uses the chroot path (`/chroot/path`) to make the data available under that particular path. This enables having the Zookeeper cluster available for multiple Kafka clusters. This path must be created before starting the Kafka cluster, and consumers must use the same string.
- `zookeeper.session.timeout.ms`: Default value: 6000. Session timeout means that if in this time period a heartbeat from the server is not received, it is considered dead. This parameter is fundamental, since if it is long and if the server is dead the whole system will experience problems. If it is small, a living server could be considered dead.
- `zookeeper.connection.timeout.ms`: Default value: 6000. This is the maximum time that the client will wait while establishing a connection to Zookeeper.
- `zookeeper.sync.time.ms`: Default value: 2000. This is the time a Zookeeper follower can be behind its Zookeeper leader.

See also

- From the Kafka perspective, the ZooKeeper parameters are detailed at: http://kafka.apache.org/documentation.html#brokerconfigs
- The Apache ZooKeeper home page is here: https://zookeeper.apache.org/

Configuring other miscellaneous parameters

No parameter should be left at default when optimal behavior is desired. These parameters should be taken into consideration to achieve the best performance.

Getting ready

With your favorite text editor, open your `server.properties` file copy.

How to do it...

Adjust the following parameters:

```
auto.create.topics.enable=true
controlled.shutdown.enable=true
controlled.shutdown.max.retries=3
controlled.shutdown.retry.backoff.ms=5000
auto.leader.rebalance.enable=true
leader.imbalance.per.broker.percentage=10
leader.imbalance.check.interval.seconds=300
offset.metadata.max.bytes=4096
max.connections.per.ip=Int.MaxValue
connections.max.idle.ms=600000
unclean.leader.election.enable=true
offsets.topic.num.partitions=50
offsets.topic.retention.minutes=1440
offsets.retention.check.interval.ms=600000
offsets.topic.replication.factor=3
offsets.topic.segment.bytes=104857600
offsets.load.buffer.size=5242880
offsets.commit.required.acks=-1
offsets.commit.timeout.ms=5000
```

How it works...

Here is an explanation of these settings:

- `auto.create.topics.enable`: Default value: true. Suppose that metadata is fetched or a message is produced for a nonexistent topic; if this value is true, the topic will automatically be created. In production environments, this value should be false.
- `controlled.shutdown.enable`: Default value: true. If this value is true, when a shutdown is called on the broker, the leader will gracefully move all the leaders to a different broker. When it is true, the availability is increased.
- `controlled.shutdown.max.retries`: Default value: 3. This is the maximum number of retries the broker tries a controlled shutdown before making a forced and unclean shutdown.
- `controlled.shutdown.retry.backoff.ms`: Default value: 5000. Suppose that a failure happens (controller fail over, replica lag, and so on); this value determines the time to wait before recovery from the state that caused the failure.
- `auto.leader.rebalance.enable`: Default value: true. If this value is true, the broker will automatically try to balance the partition leadership among the brokers. At regular intervals, a background thread checks and triggers leader balance if required, setting the leadership to the preferred replica of each partition if available.
- `leader.imbalance.per.broker.percentage`: Default value: 10. This value is specified in percentages and is the leader imbalance allowed per broker (the leader imbalance will be explained later). The cluster will rebalance the leadership if this percentage goes above the set value.
- `leader.imbalance.check.interval.seconds`: Default value: 300. This value is the frequency at which to check the leader imbalance by the controller.
- `offset.metadata.max.bytes`: Default value: 4096. This is the maximum size allowed to the client for a metadata to be stored with an offset commit.
- `max.connections.per.ip`: Default value: 2 147 483 647. This is the maximum number of connections that the broker accepts from each IP address.
- `connections.max.idle.ms`: Default value: 600 000. This is the idle connection's timeout. The server socket processor threads close the connections that idle more than this value.
- `unclean.leader.election.enable`: Default value: true. If this value is true, the replicas that are not ISR can become leaders. Doing so may result in data loss.

- `offsets.topic.num.partitions`: Default value: 50. This is the number of partitions for the offset commit topic. This value cannot be changed post deployment.
- `offsets.retention.minutes`: Default value: 1440. This is the log retention window for the offsets topic. This is the time to keep the offsets. Passed this, the offsets will be marked for deletion.
- `offsets.retention.check.interval.ms`: Default value: 60 000. This is the frequency at which to check for stale offsets
- `offsets.topic.replication.factor`: Default value: 3. This is the number of replicas for the offset commit topic. The higher this value, the higher the availability. As shown in the previous recipes, if the number of brokers is lower than the replication factor, the number of replicas will be equal to the number of brokers.
- `offsets.topic.segment.bytes`: Default value: 104 857 600. This is the segment size for the offsets topic. The lower this value, the faster the log compaction and cache loading are.
- `offsets.load.buffer.size`: Default value: 5 242 880. This is the batch size to be used for reading offset segments when loading offsets into the cache.
- `offsets.commit.required.acks`: Default value: -1. This is the number of acknowledgements required before the offset commit can be accepted. It is recommended to not override the default value of -1, meaning no acknowledgements required.
- `offsets.commit.timeout.ms`: Default value: 5000. This is the time that an offset commit will be delayed until all replicas for the offsets topic receive the commit or this time value is reached. This value is similar to the producer `request.timeout.ms`.

See also

- There are more broker configurations that are available. Read more about them at: `http://kafka.apache.org/documentation.html#brokerconfigs`

2
Kafka Clusters

In this chapter, we will cover the following topics:

- Configuring a single-node single-broker cluster – SNSB
- SNSB – creating a topic, producer, and consumer
- Configuring a single-node multiple-broker cluster – SNMB
- SNMB – creating a topic, producer, and consumer
- Configuring a multiple-node multiple-broker cluster – MNMB

Introduction

In the previous chapter, we explained how to program with the Apache Kafka publisher-subscriber messaging system. In Apache Kafka there are three types of clusters:

- Single-node single-broker
- Single-node multiple-broker
- Multiple-node multiple-broker cluster

The following four recipes show how to run Apache Kafka in these clusters.

Configuring a single-node single-broker cluster – SNSB

The first cluster configuration is **single-node single-broker** (SNSB). This cluster is very useful when a single point of entry is needed. Yes, its architecture resembles the singleton design pattern. A SNSB cluster usually satisfies three requirements:

- Controls concurrent access to a unique shared broker
- Access to the broker is requested from multiple, disparate producers
- There can be only one broker

If the proposed design has only one or two of these requirements, a redesign is almost always the correct option.

Sometimes, the single broker could become a bottleneck or a single point of failure. But it is useful when a single point of communication is needed.

Getting ready

Go to the Kafka installation directory (`/usr/local/kafka/` for macOS users and `/opt/kafka/` for Linux users):

```
> cd /usr/local/kafka
```

How to do it...

The diagram shows an example of an SNSB cluster:

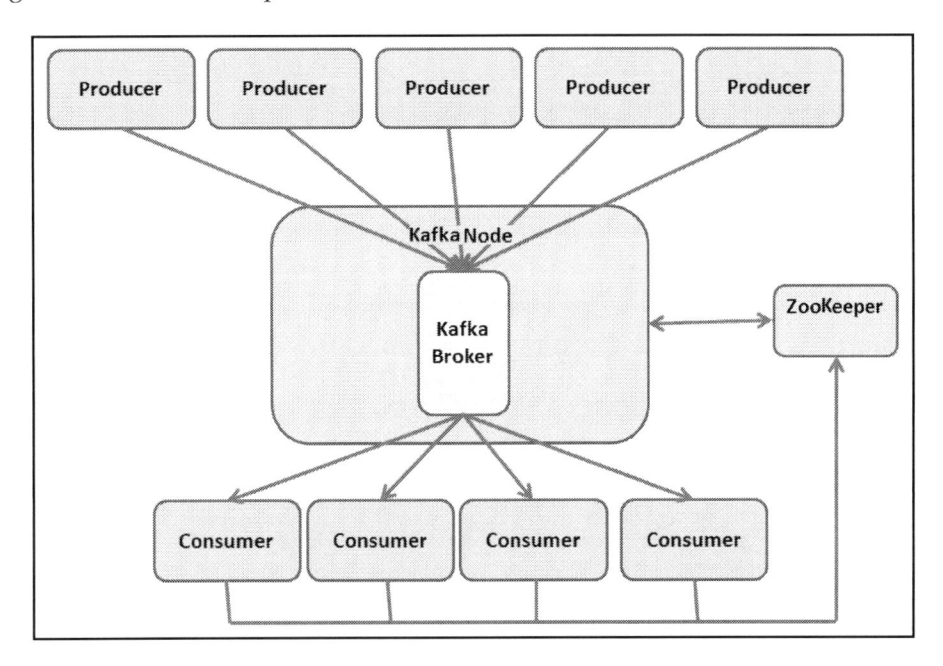

Starting ZooKeeper

1. Kafka provides a simple ZooKeeper configuration file to launch a single ZooKeeper instance. To install the ZooKeeper instance, use this command:

   ```
   > bin/zookeeper-server-start.sh config/zookeeper.properties
   ```

2. The main properties specified in the `zookeeper.properties` file are:
   - `clientPort`: This is the listening port for client requests. By default, ZooKeeper listens on TCP port `2181`:

     ```
     clientPort=2181
     ```

   - `dataDir`: This is the directory where ZooKeeper is stored:

     ```
     dataDir=/tmp/zookeeper
     ```

Kafka Clusters

- `maxClientCnxns`: The maximum number of connections per IP (0 means unbounded):

  `maxClientCnxns=0`

> For more information about Apache ZooKeeper visit the project home page at: `http://zookeeper.apache.org/`.

Starting the broker

3. After ZooKeeper is started, start the Kafka broker with this command:

   > `bin/kafka-server-start.sh config/server.properties`

4. The main properties specified in the `server.properties` file are:
   - `broker.id`: The unique positive integer identifier for each broker:

     broker.id=0

   - `log.dir`: Directory to store log files:

     log.dir=/tmp/kafka10-logs

   - `num.partitions`: The number of log partitions per topic:

     num.partitions=2

   - `port`: The port that the socket server listens on:

     port=9092

   - `zookeeper.connect`: The ZooKeeper URL connection:

     zookeeper.connect=localhost:2181

How it works...

Kafka uses ZooKeeper for storing metadata information about the brokers, topics, and partitions. Writes to ZooKeeper are performed only on changes of consumer group membership or on changes to the Kafka cluster itself.

This amount of traffic is minimal, and there is no need for a dedicated ZooKeeper ensemble for a single Kafka cluster. Actually, many deployments use a single ZooKeeper ensemble to control multiple Kafka clusters (using a `chroot` ZooKeeper path for each cluster).

There's more...

ZooKeeper must be running on the machine before starting Kafka. To avoid starting ZooKeeper every time you need to run Kafka, install it as an operating system auto start service.

See also

- The `server.properties` template (as well as the entire Kafka project) is published online at: `https://github.com/apache/kafka/blob/trunk/config/server.properties`

SNSB – creating a topic, producer, and consumer

The SNSB Kafka cluster is running; now let's create topics, producer, and consumer.

Getting ready

We need the previous recipe executed:

- Kafka already installed
- ZooKeeper up and running

- A Kafka server up and running
- Now, go to the Kafka installation directory (`/usr/local/kafka/` for macOS users and `/opt/kafka/` for Linux users):

```
> cd /usr/local/kafka
```

How to do it...

The following steps will show you how to create an SNSB topic, producer, and consumer.

Creating a topic

1. As we know, Kafka has a command to create topics. Here we create a topic called `SNSBTopic` with one partition and one replica:

    ```
    > bin/kafka-topics.sh --create --zookeeper localhost:2181 --replication-factor 1 --partitions 1 --topic SNSBTopic
    ```

    We obtain the following output:

    ```
    Created topic "SNSBTopic".
    ```

    The command parameters are:

    - `--replication-factor 1`: This indicates just one replica
    - `--partition 1`: This indicates just one partition
    - `--zookeeper localhost:2181`: This indicates the ZooKeeper URL

2. As we know, to get the list of topics on a Kafka server we use the following command:

    ```
    > bin/kafka-topics.sh --list --zookeeper localhost:2181
    ```

    We obtain the following output:

    ```
    SNSBTopic
    ```

Starting the producer

3. Kafka has a command to start producers that accepts inputs from the command line and publishes each input line as a message. By default, each new line is considered a message:

   ```
   > bin/kafka-console-producer.sh --broker-list localhost:9092 --topic SNSBTopic
   ```

   This command requires two parameters:

   - `broker-list`: The broker URL to connect to
   - `topic`: The topic name (to send a message to the topic subscribers)

4. Now, type the following in the command line:

   ```
   The best thing about a boolean is [Enter]
   even if you are wrong [Enter]
   you are only off by a bit. [Enter]
   ```

   This output is obtained (as expected):

   ```
   The best thing about a boolean is
   even if you are wrong
   you are only off by a bit.
   ```

The `producer.properties` file has the producer configuration. Some important properties defined in the `producer.properties` file are:

- `metadata.broker.list`: The list of brokers used for bootstrapping information on the rest of the cluster in the format `host1:port1, host2:port2`:

  ```
  metadata.broker.list=localhost:9092
  ```

- `compression.codec`: The compression codec used. For example, `none`, `gzip`, and `snappy`:

  ```
  compression.codec=none
  ```

Starting the consumer

5. Kafka has a command to start a message consumer client. It shows the output in the command line as soon as it has subscribed to the topic:

    ```
    > bin/kafka-console-consumer.sh --zookeeper localhost:2181 --topic SNSBTopic --from-beginning
    ```

    Note that the parameter `from-beginning` is to show the entire log:

    ```
    The best thing about a boolean is
    even if you are wrong
    you are only off by a bit.
    ```

One important property defined in the `consumer.properties` file is:

- `group.id`: This string identifies the consumers in the same group:

    ```
    group.id=test-consumer-group
    ```

How it works...

In this recipe, a topic, a producer, and a consumer were created to test the SNSB cluster created in the previous recipe.

There's more...

It is time to play with this technology. Open a new command-line window for ZooKeeper, a broker, two producers, and two consumers. Type some messages in the producers and watch them get displayed in the consumers. If you don't know or don't remember how to run the commands, run it with no arguments to display the possible values for the parameters.

Configuring a single-node multiple-broker cluster – SNMB

The second cluster configuration is **single-node multiple-broker** (**SNMB**). This cluster is used when there is just one node but inner redundancy is needed.

When a topic is created in Kafka, the system determines how each replica of a partition is mapped to each broker. In general, Kafka tries to spread the replicas across all available brokers.

The messages are first sent to the first replica of a partition (to the current broker leader of that partition) before they are replicated to the remaining brokers.

The producers may choose from different strategies for sending messages (synchronous or asynchronous mode). Producers discover the available brokers in a cluster and the partitions on each (all this by registering watchers in ZooKeeper).

In practice, some of the high volume topics are configured with more than one partition per broker. Remember that having more partitions increases the I/O parallelism for writes and this increases the degree of parallelism for consumers (the partition is the unit for distributing data to consumers).

On the other hand, increasing the number of partitions increases the overhead because:

- There are more files, so more open file handlers
- There are more offsets to be checked by consumers, so the ZooKeeper load is increased

The art of this is to balance these tradeoffs.

Getting ready

Go to the Kafka installation directory (`/usr/local/kafka/` for macOS users and `/opt/kafka/` for Linux users):

```
> cd /usr/local/kafka
```

Kafka Clusters

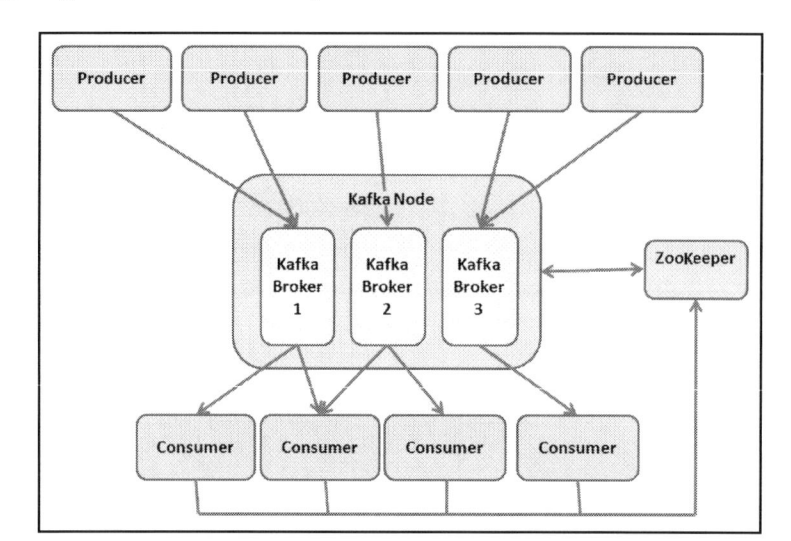

The following diagram shows an example of an SNMB cluster:

How to do it...

1. Begin starting the ZooKeeper server as follows:

   > `bin/zookeeper-server-start.sh config/zookeeper.properties`

   A different `server.properties` file is needed for each broker. Let's call them: `server-1.properties`, `server-2.properties`, `server-3.properties`, and so on (original, isn't it?).

   Each file is a copy of the original `server.properties` file.

2. In the `server-1.properties` file set the following properties:
   - `broker.id=1`
   - `port=9093`
   - `log.dir=/tmp/kafka-logs-1`

3. Similarly, in the `server-2.properties` file set the following properties:
   - `broker.id=2`
   - `port=9094`
   - `log.dir=/tmp/kafka-logs-2`

4. Finally, in the `server-3.properties` file set the following properties:
   - `broker.id=3`
   - `port=9095`
   - `log.dir=/tmp/kafka-logs-3`

5. With ZooKeeper running, start the Kafka brokers with these commands:

   ```
   > bin/kafka-server-start.sh config/server-1.properties
   > bin/kafka-server-start.sh config/server-2.properties
   > bin/kafka-server-start.sh config/server-3.properties
   ```

How it works...

Now the SNMB cluster is running. The brokers are running on the same Kafka node, on ports 9093, 9094, and 9095.

There's more...

In the following recipe, an explanation of how to create a topic, a producer, and consumer is given.

See also

- In case of file deletion, the original file is located at:
  https://github.com/apache/kafka/blob/trunk/config/server.properties

SNMB – creating a topic, producer, and consumer

The SNMB Kafka cluster is running; now let's create topics, producer, and consumer.

Getting ready

We need the previous recipe executed:

- Kafka already installed
- ZooKeeper up and running
- A Kafka server up and running
- Now, go to the Kafka installation directory (`/usr/local/kafka/` for macOS users and `/opt/kafka/` for Linux users):

```
> cd /usr/local/kafka
```

How to do it...

The following steps will show you how to create an SNMB topic, producer, and consumer

Creating a topic

1. Using the command to create topics, let's create a topic called `SNMBTopic` with two partitions and two replicas:

    ```
    > bin/kafka-topics.sh --create --zookeeper localhost:2181 --replication-factor 2 --partitions 3 --topic SNMBTopic
    ```

    The following output is displayed:

    ```
    Created topic "SNMBTopic".
    ```

    This command has the following effects:

    - Kafka will create three logical partitions for the topic.
    - Kafka will create two replicas (copies) per partition. This means, for each partition it will pick two brokers that will host those replicas. For each partition, Kafka will randomly choose a broker leader.

2. Now ask Kafka for the list of available topics. The list now includes the new SNMBTopic:

   ```
   > bin/kafka-topics.sh --zookeeper localhost:2181 --list
   SNMBTopic
   ```

Starting a producer

3. Now, start the producers; indicating more brokers in the `broker-list` is easy:

   ```
   > bin/kafka-console-producer.sh --broker-list localhost:9093,
   localhost:9094, localhost:9095 --topic SNMBTopic
   ```

   If it's necessary to run multiple producers connecting to different brokers, specify a different broker list for each producer.

Starting a consumer

4. To start a consumer, use the following command:

```
> bin/kafka-console-consumer.sh -- zookeeper localhost:2181 --from-
beginning --topic SNMBTopic
```

How it works...

The first important fact is the two parameters: `replication-factor` and `partitions`.

The `replication-factor` is the number of replicas each partition will have in the topic created.

The `partitions` parameter is the number of partitions for the topic created.

There's more...

If you don't know the cluster configuration or don't remember it, there is a useful option for the `kafka-topics` command, the `describe` parameter:

```
> bin/kafka-topics.sh --zookeeper localhost:2181 --describe --topic
SNMBTopic
```

The output is something similar to:

```
Topic:SNMBTopic        PartitionCount:3   ReplicationFactor:2   Configs:
    Topic: SNMBTopic   Partition: 0       Leader: 2    Replicas: 2,3     Isr: 3,2
    Topic: SNMBTopic   Partition: 1       Leader: 3    Replicas: 3,1     Isr: 1,3
    Topic: SNMBTopic   Partition: 2       Leader: 1    Replicas: 1,2     Isr: 1,2
```

An explanation of the output: the first line gives a summary of all the partitions; each line gives information about one partition. Since we have three partitions for this topic, there are three lines:

- `Leader`: This node is responsible for all reads and writes for a particular partition. For a randomly selected section of the partitions each node is the leader.
- `Replicas`: This is the list of nodes that duplicate the log for a particular partition irrespective of whether it is currently alive.
- `Isr`: This is the set of in-sync replicas. It is a subset of the replicas currently alive and following the leader.

See also

- In order to see the options for: create, delete, describe, or change a topic, type this command without parameters:

    ```
    > bin/kafka-topics.sh
    ```

Configuring a multiple-node multiple-broker cluster – MNMB

Finally, the third cluster configuration is **multiple-node multiple-broker** (**MNMB**). This cluster is used when there are several nodes and one or many brokers per node.

Chapter 2

Getting ready

Go to the Kafka installation directory (`/usr/local/kafka/` for macOS users and `/opt/kafka/` for Linux users):

```
> cd /usr/local/kafka
```

How to do it...

The following diagram shows an example MNMB cluster:

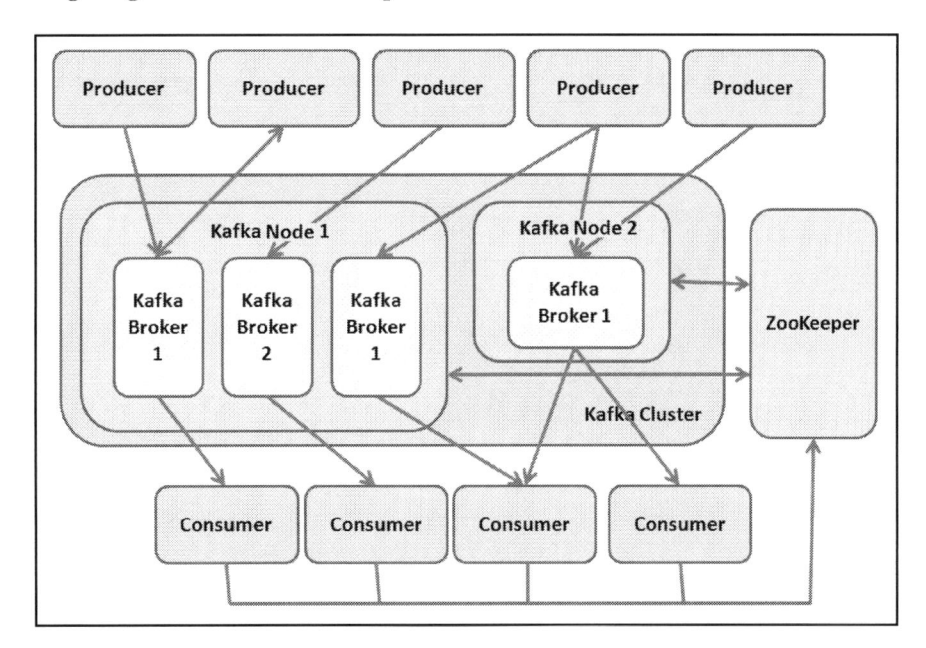

Here we are presented with the real power of the cluster. In this cluster, Kafka should be installed on every machine in the cluster. Here, every physical server could have one or many brokers; all the nodes on the same cluster should connect to the same ZooKeeper.

How it works...

The good news is that all the commands in the previous recipes remain the same. The commands for ZooKeeper, the broker, producer, and consumer, don't change.

See also

- The complete list of important properties of Kafka brokers is at: http://kafka.apache.org/documentation.html#brokerconfigs

3
Message Validation

In this chapter, we cover the following topics:

- Modeling the events
- Setting up the project
- Reading from Kafka
- Writing to Kafka
- Running ProcessingApp
- Coding the validator
- Running the validator

Introduction

The first two chapters were focused on how to build a Kafka cluster, run a producer, and run a consumer. Now that we have a producer of events, we will process those events.

In a nutshell, event processing takes one or more events from an event stream and applies actions to those events. In general, an enterprise service bus has commodity services, the most common services are the following:

- Event handling
- Data transformation
- Data mapping
- Protocol conversion

The operation of processing events involves the following:

- An event stream to filter some events from the stream
- Event validation against an event schema
- Event enrichment with additional data
- Event composition (aggregation) to produce a new event from two or more events

This chapter is about message validation, the following chapters will be about enrichment and composition.

Before going into a concrete recipe, let's present a case study. Imagine that we are modeling the systems of Doubloon, a fictional company dedicated to cryptocurrency exchange. Doubloon wants to implement an enterprise service bus with Apache Kafka. The goal is to unify all of the logs in its business. Doubloon has a website, the objective is to react to customer behavior in a timely way.

Worldwide, online customers browse the Doubloon website to exchange their currencies. There are a lot of other things that visitors can do on the website, but we will focus on the exchange rate query workflow, specifically from the web application.

Modeling the events

This recipe shows how to model events in JSON format.

Getting ready

For this recipe, basic knowledge of JSON is required.

How to do it...

The first step to model an event is expressing it in English language in the form: *subject-verb-direct object*.

For this example, we are going to model the event *customer sees BTC price*:

- **Customer**: This is the sentence's subject, a noun in nominative case. The subject in an English sentence is the entity performing the action.

- **Sees**: This is the verb of the sentence, it describes the action being done by the subject.
- **BTC price**: This is the direct object of the sentence or simply the object. The entity to which the action is being done.

There are several options for data representation, in this case we will pick JSON. We could use Avro, Apache Thrift, or Protocol Buffers, but they will be covered in later chapters.

JSON has the advantage of being easily read and written by both humans and machines. For example, one could use binary as representation, but it is not easily read by humans and has a very rigid format; on the other hand, binary representation is light in weight.

The following snippet shows the representation of the *customer sees BTC price* event in JSON:

```
{
  "event": "CUSTOMER_SEES_BTCPRICE",
  "customer": {
    "id": "86689427",
    "name": "Edward S.",
    "ipAddress": "95.31.18.119"
  },
  "currency": {
    "name": "bitcoin",
    "price": "USD"
  },
  "timestamp": "2017-07-03T12:00:35Z"
}
```

How it works...

Yes, the solution sometimes raises more questions than answers. In this case, we see the currency price expressed in dollars, why? Well, the proposed representation of this event in JSON has four properties:

- `event`: This is a string with the event's name.
- `customer`: This represents the person (in this case, his name is `Edward`) viewing the bitcoin price. In this representation, there is a unique ID for the customer, his name, and the browser IP address, which is the IP address of the computer he is browsing on.

Message Validation

- `currency`: This contains the name and the currency in which the price is expressed.
- `timestamp`: This is fundamental because it is the time the customer sent the request in seconds.

Let's analyze the event from another perspective. The event has only two parts: the metadata, namely the `event`, `name`, and the `timestamp`; and two business entities, the `customer` and the `currency`. As one can see, this message can be read and understood by a human.

There's more...

We can represent this message schema. This is the template of all the messages of this type in Avro. Our message in Avro schema would be as follows:

```
{ "name": "customer_sees_btcprice",
  "namespace": "doubloon.avro",
  "type": "record",
  "fields": [
    { "name": "event", "type": "string" },
    { "name": "customer",
      "type": {
        "name": "id", "type": "long",
        "name": "name", "type": "string",
        "name": "ipAddress", "type": "string"
      }
    },
    { "name": "currency",
      "type": {
        "name": "name", "type": "string",
        "name": "price", "type": {
          "type": "enum", "namespace": "doubloon.avro",
          "name": "priceEnum", "symbols": ["USD", "EUR"]}
      }
    },
    { "name": "timestamp", "type": "long",
      "logicalType": "timestamp-millis"
    }
  ]
}
```

In the following recipes, we also use these messages:

```
{   "event": "CUSTOMER_SEES_BTCPRICE",
    "customer": {
      "id": "18313440",
      "name": "Julian A.",
      "ipAddress": "185.86.151.11"
    },
    "currency": {
      "name": "bitcoin",
      "price": "USD"
    },
    "timestamp": "2017-07-04T15:00:35Z"
}
```

We also use the following messages:

```
{   "event": "CUSTOMER_SEES_BTCPRICE",
    "customer": {
      "id": "56886468",
      "name": "Lindsay M.",
      "ipAddress": "186.46.129.15"
    },
    "currency": {
      "name": "bitcoin",
      "price": "USD"
    },
    "timestamp": "2017-07-11T19:00:35Z"
}
```

See also

- For more information about schemas, check the Apache Avro specification at: http://avro.apache.org/docs/current

Message Validation

Setting up the project

Before writing code, let's remember the project requirements for the stream processing application. Recall that *customer sees BTC price* events happen in the customer's web browser and are dispatched to Kafka via an HTTP event collector. Events are created in an environment out of the control of Doubloon. The first step is to validate that the input events have the correct structure. Remember that defective events could create bad data (most data scientists agree that a lot of time could be saved if input data were clean).

Getting ready

Putting it all together, the specification is to create a stream application which does the following:

- Reads individual events from a Kafka topic called **raw-messages**
- Validates the event, sending any invalid message to a dedicated Kafka topic called **invalid-messages**
- *Writes* the correct events to a Kafka topic called **valid-messages**, and writes corrupted messages to an **invalid-messages** topic

All this is detailed in the following diagram, the first sketch of our stream processing application:

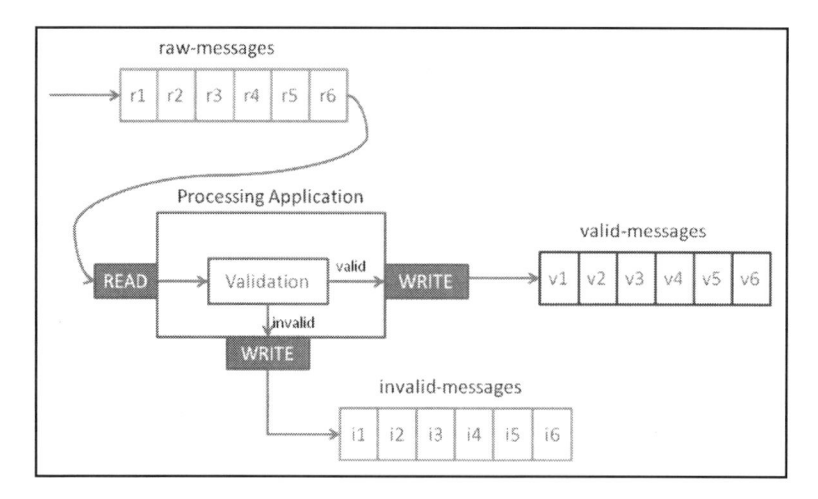

Figure 3.1: The processing application reads events from the raw-messages topic, validates the messages, and routes the errors to the invalid-messages topic and the correct ones to the valid-messages topic

How to do it...

There are two steps in the stream processing application:

1. Create a simple Kafka worker that reads from the raw-messages topic in Kafka and writes the events to a new topic
2. Modify the Kafka worker to handle the validation

The first step is to download and install Gradle from: http://www.gradle.org/downloads. Gradle requires only a Java JDK or JDE version 7 or above. We can install Gradle in the following ways:

- For macOS users, the `brew` command will be enough:

    ```
    $ brew update && brew install gradle
    ```

- For Linux users, we use `apt-get`:

```
$ sudo apt-get install gradle
```

- For Unix users, we use SDKMAN, a tool for managing parallel versions of most Unix-based systems:

    ```
    $ sdk install gradle 4.3
    ```

The manual installation steps are as follows:

1. Download the latest version from http://www.gradle.org/downloads and select binary only. The latest version as of now is 4.3.
2. Unpack the distribution:

    ```
    $ mkdir /opt/gradle
    $ unzip /opt/gradle gradle-4.3-bin.zip
    $ ls /opt/gradle/gradle-4.3
    LICENSE   NOTICE   bin   getting-started.html   init.d   lib   media
    ```

3. Configure your system environment:

    ```
    $ export PATH=$PATH:/opt/gradle/gradle-4.3/bin
    ```

Message Validation

4. Finally, to check that Gradle is installed correctly, type the following:

   ```
   $ gradle -v
   ```

   The output is something like the following:

   ```
   ------------------------------------------------------------
   Gradle 4.3
   ------------------------------------------------------------
   ```

The next step is to create our project with Gradle, which will be called `ProcessingApp`.

1. Create a directory called `doubloon`, go to that directory, and execute the following:

   ```
   $ gradle init --type java-library
   ```

   The output is something like the following:

   ```
   ...
   BUILD SUCCESSFUL
   ...
   ```

2. Gradle creates a skeleton project in the directory, with two Java files called `Library.java` and `LibraryTest.java`. Feel free to delete both files. Your directory should be similar to the following:

   ```
   - build.gradle
   - gradle
   -- wrapper
   --- gradle-wrapper.jar
   --- gradle-vreapper.properties
   - gradlew
   - gradle.bat
   - settings.gradle
   - src
   -- main
   --- java
   ----- Library.java
   -- test
   --- java
   ----- LibraryTest.java
   ```

[64]

3. Now, modify the Gradle build file called `build.gradle` and replace with the following code:

```
apply plugin: 'java'
apply plugin: 'application'

sourceCompatibility = '1.8'

mainClassName = 'doubloon.ProcessingApp'

repositories {
  mavenCentral()
}

version = '0.1.0'

dependencies {
  compile 'org.apache.kafka:kafka-clients:0.11.0.1'
  compile 'com.fasterxml.jackson.core:jackson-databind:2.6.3'
}
jar {
manifest {
  attributes 'Main-Class': mainClassName
  }
  from {
    configurations.compile.collect {
      it.isDirectory() ? it : zipTree(it)
    }
  } {
    exclude "META-INF/*.SF"
    exclude "META-INF/*.DSA"
    exclude "META-INF/*.RSA"
  }
}
```

How it works...

Some library dependencies were added to the application:

- `kafka_2.11`: This is a necessary dependency for Apache Kafka
- `jackson-databind`: This is the library for JSON parsing and manipulation

Message Validation

To compile the sources and download the required libraries, type the following command:

```
$ gradle compileJava
```

The output should be as follows:

```
...
BUILD SUCCESSFUL
...
```

There's more...

The project can be created with Maven or SBT, even from the IDE, but for simplicity, here we created it with Gradle.

See also

- Gradle's main page: http://www.gradle.org
- Maven's main page: http://maven.apache.org
- SBT's main page: http://www.scala-sbt.org/

Reading from Kafka

The next step is to read individual raw messages from the Kafka topic, raw-messages. In Kafka jargon, a consumer is needed. In the last chapter, we used the command-line tools to write events to a topic and to read events back to the topic. This recipe shows how to write a Kafka consumer in Java using the Kafka library.

Getting ready

The execution of the previous recipes in this chapter is needed.

How to do it...

1. Create a file called `Consumer.java` in the `src/main/java/doubloon/` directory with the following code:

   ```
   package doubloon;

   import java.util.Properties;

   import org.apache.kafka.clients.consumer.ConsumerRecords;

   public interface Consumer {
       public static Properties createConfig(String servers, String groupId) {
           Properties props = new Properties();
           props.put("bootstrap.servers", servers);
           props.put("group.id", groupId);
           props.put("enable.auto.commit", "true");
           props.put("auto.commit.interval.ms", "1000");
           props.put("auto.offset.reset", "earliest");
           props.put("session.timeout.ms", "30000");
           props.put("key.deserializer",
   "org.apache.kafka.common.serialization.StringDeserializer");
           props.put("value.deserializer",
   "org.apache.kafka.common.serialization.StringDeserializer");
           return props;
       }

       public ConsumerRecords<String, String> consume();
   }
   ```

   The `Consumer` interface encapsulates the common behavior of all the Kafka consumers. Principally, the `Consumer` interface has the `createConfig` method, which sets all the properties needed by the consumers. Note that `deserializers` are of the `StringDeserializer` type because the Kafka consumer reads Kafka records, where the key and value are both of `String` type. The `consume` is a method that would be implemented by `Reader` class.

2. Now, create a file called `Reader.java` in the `src/main/java/doubloon/` directory with the following code:

   ```
   package doubloon;

   import org.apache.kafka.clients.consumer.ConsumerRecords;
   import org.apache.kafka.clients.consumer.KafkaConsumer;
   ```

Message Validation

```java
public class Reader implements Consumer {

    private final KafkaConsumer<String, String> consumer; // 1
    private final String topic;

    public Reader(String servers, String groupId, String topic) {
        this.consumer = new KafkaConsumer<String, String>(Consumer.createConfig(servers, groupId));
        this.topic = topic;
    }

    @Override
    public ConsumerRecords<String, String> consume() {
        this.consumer.subscribe(java.util.Arrays.asList(this.topic)); // 2
        ConsumerRecords<String, String> records = consumer.poll(100); // 3
        return records;
    }
}
```

How it works...

The `Reader` implements the `Consumer` interface. So, the reader is a Kafka consumer.

As said, in line 1, `<String, String>` says that this Kafka consumer reads Kafka records where the key and value are both of `String` type. In line 2, the `Consumer` subscribes to the Kafka topic specified in the constructor. In line 3, the poll will fetch the data for the topics or partitions specified with a timeout of 100 milliseconds.

This `Consumer` reads records from the Kafka topic given and sends them to the calling method. All the configuration properties are specified in the `Consumer` interface, but the `groupId` property is especially important because it lets us associate this `Consumer` with a specific consumer group.

The consumer group is useful when one needs to share out the topic's events across all the group's members. On the other hand, consumer groups are also used to group or isolate different instances.

There's more...

Now we have the reader, in the next recipe let's code the writer because the writer is nothing without readers.

See also

- To read more about the Kafka consumer API, visit: https://kafka.apache.org/0110/javadoc/index.html and search for KafkaConsumer in the lower-left of the UI

Writing to Kafka

In the last recipe, the Reader has the invocation of the process method. This method belongs to the Producer class. In this recipe, the Writer class is explained.

Getting ready

The execution of the previous recipes in this chapter is needed.

How to do it...

As we did with the Consumer interface, the Producer interface is needed to keep things flexible. The two producers in this chapter will implement the Producer interface. This interface isolates all the common behavior of the producers.

Copy the following content to a file called src/main/java/doubloon/Producer.java:

```
package doubloon;

import java.util.Properties;

public interface Producer {

    public void produce(String message); // 1

    public static Properties createConfig(String servers) { // 2
        Properties props = new Properties();
        props.put("bootstrap.servers", servers);
        props.put("acks", "all");
        props.put("retries", 0);
        props.put("batch.size", 1000);
        props.put("linger.ms", 1);
        props.put("key.serializer",
"org.apache.kafka.common.serialization.StringSerializer");
```

Message Validation

```
        props.put("value.serializer",
"org.apache.kafka.common.serialization.StringSerializer");
        return props;
    }
}
```

The `Producer` interface has the following details:

- In line 1, the `produce` method is implemented in the `Writer` class, which sends a message to the producer in the topic specified.
- In line 2, a static method called `createConfig`, as its consumer counterpart, sets the properties needed for a generic producer

Now, as with the consumer, an implementation of the `Producer` interface is needed. In this first version, we just send the incoming source messages through into a second topic with the messages untouched. The following implementation code should be saved in a file called `src/main/java/doubloon/Writer.java`:

```
package doubloon;

import org.apache.kafka.clients.producer.*;

public class Writer implements Producer {

    private final KafkaProducer<String, String> producer;
    private final String topic;

    public Writer(String servers, String topic) {
        this.producer = new KafkaProducer<String,
String>(Producer.createConfig(servers)); // 1
        this.topic = topic;
    }

    @Override
    public void produce(String message) { //2
        ProducerRecord<String, String> pr = new ProducerRecord<String,
String>(topic, message);
        producer.send(pr);
    }
}
```

How it works...

In this implementation we have the following:

- In line 1, the `createConfig` method is invoked to set the necessary properties from the `Producer` interface.
- In line 2, the `produce` method just writes the incoming messages in the output topic. As the message arrives to the topic, it is copied to the target topic.

This `Producer` implementation is self-explanatory. It doesn't change, validate, or enrich the incoming messages, it just writes them to the target topic.

There's more...

Now we have the reader and the writer, in the next recipe let's run everything.

See also

- To read more about the Kafka Producer API, visit: `https://kafka.apache.org/0110/javadoc/index.html` and search for KafkaProducer in the lower-left of the UI

Running ProcessingApp

In the last recipe, the `Writer` class was coded. Now, in this recipe everything is compiled and executed.

Getting ready

The execution of the previous recipes in this chapter is needed.

Message Validation

How to do it...

The `ProcessingApp` class coordinates the `Reader` and `Writer` classes. It contains the `main` method to execute them. Create a new file called `src/main/java/doubloon/ProcessingApp.java` and fill it with the following code:

```java
package doubloon;

import org.apache.kafka.clients.consumer.ConsumerRecord;
import org.apache.kafka.clients.consumer.ConsumerRecords;

public class ProcessingApp {

    public static void main(String[] args) {
        String servers = args[0];
        String groupId = args[1];
        String sourceTopic = args[2];
        String targetTopic = args[3];

        Reader reader = new Reader(servers, groupId, sourceTopic);
        Writer writer = new Writer(servers, targetTopic);

        while (true) { // 1
            ConsumerRecords<String, String> consumeRecords = reader.consume();
            for (ConsumerRecord<String, String> record : consumeRecords) {
                writer.produce(record.value()); // 2
            }
        }
    }
}
```

How it works...

The `ProcessingApp` receives four arguments from the command line:

- `args[0] servers`: This specifies the host and port of the Kafka broker
- `args[1] group id`: This specifies that the `Consumer` belongs to this Kafka consumer group
- `args[2] source topic`: This is the topic `Reader` will read from
- `args[3] target topic`: This is the topic `Writer` will write to

In line 1, yes, some people are afraid to do `while(true)` loops, but in this example it is necessary for demonstrative purposes. In line 2 we send every message to be processed by the `Producer`

To build the project, from the `doubloon` directory, run the following command:

```
$ gradle jar
```

If everything is okay, the output should be as follows:

```
...
BUILD SUCCESSFUL
Total time: ...
```

To run the project, open six different command-line windows. The following diagram shows what the command-line windows should look like:

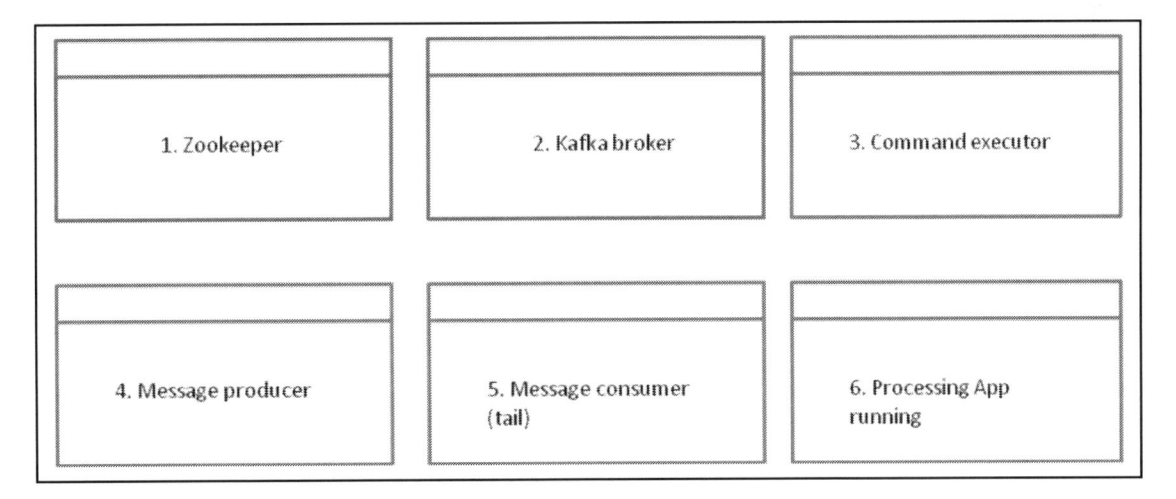

| 1. Zookeeper | 2. Kafka broker | 3. Command executor |
| 4. Message producer | 5. Message consumer (tail) | 6. Processing App running |

Figure 3.2: The six terminals to test the processing application include Zookeeper, Kafka broker, Command executor, Message producer, Message consumer, and the application itself

In the first command-line Terminal, move to the Kafka installation directory and type the following:

```
$ bin/zookeeper-server-start.sh config/zookeeper.properties
```

In the second command-line Terminal, go to the Kafka installation directory and type the following:

```
$ bin/kafka-server-start.sh config/server.properties
```

Message Validation

In the third command-line Terminal, go to the Kafka installation directory and generate the two necessary topics:

- $ bin/kafka-topics.sh --create --zookeeper localhost:2181 --replication-factor 1 --partitions 1 --topic source-topic
- $ bin/kafka-topics.sh --create --zookeeper localhost:2181 --replication-factor 1 --partitions 1 --topic target-topic

Remember that the parameter list shows the existing topics as follows:

$ bin/kafka-topics.sh --list --zookeeper localhost:2181

Also remember that to delete an unwanted topic (yes, everybody makes mistakes) we do the following:

$ bin/kafka-topics.sh --delete --zookeeper localhost:2181 --topic unWantedTopic

In the fourth command-line Terminal, start the broker running the source-topic topic:

$ bin/kafka-console-producer.sh --broker-list localhost:9092 --topic source-topic

The preceding window is where the input messages are typed.

In the fifth command-line Terminal, start a consumer script listening to target-topic:

$ bin/kafka-console-consumer.sh --bootstrap-server localhost:9092 --from-beginning --topic target-topic

In the sixth command-line Terminal, start up the processing application. Go to the project root directory (where the Gradle jar command was executed) and run the following:

$ java -jar ./build/libs/doubloon-0.1.0.jar localhost:9092 vipConsumersGroup source-topic target-topic

Now, that we have the stages mounted, the magic is about to happen. This act consists of reading all the events from the source-topic and writing them into the target-topic.

Go to the fourth command-line Terminal (the console producer) and send the following three messages (remember to press *Enter* between messages and execute each one in just one line):

```
{"event": "CUSTOMER_SEES_BTCPRICE", "customer": {"id": "86689427", "name": "Edward S.", "ipAddress": "95.31.18.119"}, "currency": {"name": "bitcoin", "price": "USD"}, "timestamp": "2017-07-03T12:00:35Z"}

{"event": "CUSTOMER_SEES_BTCPRICE", "customer": {"id": "18313440", "name": "Julian A.", "ipAddress": "185.86.151.11"}, "currency": {"name": "bitcoin", "price": "USD"}, "timestamp": "2017-07-04T15:00:35Z"}

{"event": "CUSTOMER_SEES_BTCPRICE", "customer": {"id": "56886468", "name": "Lindsay M.", "ipAddress": "186.46.129.15"}, "currency": {"name": "bitcoin", "price": "USD"}, "timestamp": "2017-07-11T19:00:35Z"}
```

If everything works fine, the messages typed in the console-producer should be appearing in the console-consumer window.

There's more...

The next step is to move onto a more complex version involving message validation (later in this chapter), message enrichment (next chapter), and message transformation (two chapters forward).

For the next recipe, shut down the processing application (with *Ctrl* + *Z* in the sixth terminal), but don't close any other terminals.

See also

- As we can see, the replication-factor and partitions parameters where set to 1. Now, try playing with different values. `Chapter 8`, *Operating Kafka* is dedicated entirely to this kind of parameterization.

Coding the validator

The next recipe involves the evolution from a simple Kafka producer-consumer to a Kafka message stream processor that includes validation and routing.

Getting ready

The execution of the previous recipes in this chapter are needed.

How to do it...

Good architecture implies flexibility. As shown in the *Writting* recipe, the `Writer` class implements the `Producer` interface. The idea is to start with that `Writer` and build a more sophisticated class with minimum effort. Let's recall the goals for our `Validator`:

- Read the Kafka messages from the source-messages topic
- Validate the messages, sending the defective messages to a different topic
- Write the good messages to the good-messages topic

For simplicity, the definition of a valid message is a message that is as follows:

- In JSON format
- Contains the four required fields: `event`, `customer`, `currency`, and `timestamp`

If these conditions aren't met, a new error message in JSON format is generated, sending it to the bad events Kafka topic. The schema of this error message is very simple:

```
{"error": "Failure description" }
```

The first step is to copy the following code to the `src/main/java/doubloon/Validator.java` file:

```java
package doubloon;

import java.io.IOException;

import org.apache.kafka.clients.producer.KafkaProducer;
import org.apache.kafka.clients.producer.ProducerRecord;

import com.fasterxml.jackson.databind.JsonNode;
import com.fasterxml.jackson.databind.ObjectMapper;

public class Validator implements Producer {

    private final KafkaProducer<String, String> producer;
    private final String goodTopic;
    private final String badTopic;
```

```java
    protected static final ObjectMapper MAPPER = new ObjectMapper();

    public Validator(String servers, String goodTopic, String badTopic) {
// 1
        this.producer = new KafkaProducer<String,
String>(Producer.createConfig(servers));
        this.goodTopic = goodTopic;
        this.badTopic = badTopic;
    }

    @Override
    public void produce(String message) { //2
        ProducerRecord<String, String> pr = null;
        try {
            JsonNode root = MAPPER.readTree(message);
            String error = "";
            error = error.concat(validate(root, "event"));
            error = error.concat(validate(root, "customer"));
            error = error.concat(validate(root, "currency"));
            error = error.concat(validate(root, "timestamp"));
            // TO_DO: implement for the inner children

            if (error.length() > 0) {
                pr = new ProducerRecord<String, String>(this.badTopic,
"{\"error\": \" " + error + "\"}"); // 3
            } else {
                pr = new ProducerRecord<String, String>(this.goodTopic,
MAPPER.writeValueAsString(root));// 4
            }
        } catch (IOException e) {
            pr = new ProducerRecord<String, String>(this.badTopic,
                    "{\"error\": \"" + e.getClass().getSimpleName() + ": "
+ e.getMessage() + "\"}"); // 5
        } finally {
            if (null != pr) {
                producer.send(pr);
            }
        }
    }

    private String validate(JsonNode root, String path) {
        if (!root.has(path)) {
            return path.concat(" is missing. ");
        }

        JsonNode node = root.path(path);
        if (node.isMissingNode()) {
            return path.concat(" is missing. ");
```

Message Validation

```
            }
            return "";
        }
    }
```

The `Validator` class has the following details:

- In line 1, the constructor takes two topics: the good and the bad message topics
- In line 2, the `produce` method validates that the message is in JSON format, and the existence of the `event`, `customer`, `currency`, and `timestamp` fields
- In line 3, if the message doesn't have any required fields, an error message is sent to the bad messages topic
- In line 4, if the message is correct, the message is sent to the good messages topic
- In line 5, if the message is not in JSON format, an error message is sent to the bad messages topic

There's more...

Your turn... there is a to-do comment, you have to implement the validation of the node inner children, not just the four main nodes.

See also

- All the validation architecture is detailed in the first diagram of this chapter

Running the validator

In the last recipe, the `Validator` class was coded. Now, in this recipe everything is compiled and executed.

Getting ready

The execution of the previous recipes in this chapter are needed.

How to do it...

At this point, the `ProcessingApp` class coordinates the `Reader` and `Writer` classes. It contains the `main` method to execute them. We have to edit the `ProcessingApp.java` file located at `src/main/java/doubloon/ProcessingApp.java` and change it with the following code:

```java
package doubloon;

import org.apache.kafka.clients.consumer.ConsumerRecord;
import org.apache.kafka.clients.consumer.ConsumerRecords;

public class ProcessingApp {

    public static void main(String[] args) {
        String servers = args[0];
        String groupId = args[1];
        String sourceTopic = args[2];
        String goodTopic = args[3];
        String badTopic = args[4];

        Reader reader = new Reader(servers, groupId, sourceTopic);
        Validator validator = new Validator(servers, goodTopic, badTopic);

        while (true) {
            ConsumerRecords<String, String> consumeRecords =
reader.consume();
            for (ConsumerRecord<String, String> record : consumeRecords) {
                validator.produce(record.value());
            }
        }
    }
}
```

How it works...

The `ProcessingApp` now receives five arguments from the command line:

- `args[0] servers`: This specifies the host and port of the Kafka broker
- `args[1] group id`: This specifies that the consumer belongs to this Kafka consumer group
- `args[2] source topic`: This is the topic the reader will read from

Message Validation

- `args[3] good topic`: This is the topic the good messages will be sent to
- `args[4] bad topic`: This is the topic the bad messages will be sent to

To build the project, from the `doubloon` directory, run the following command:

```
$ gradle jar
```

If everything is okay, the output should be as follows:

```
...
BUILD SUCCESSFUL
Total time: ...
```

To run the project, we have the six different command-line windows from the previous recipes. The following diagram shows what the arrangement of command-line windows should look like:

1. ZooKeeper	2. Kafka broker	3. Message producer
4. Good Message consumer (tail)	5. Bad Message consumer (tail)	6. Processing App running

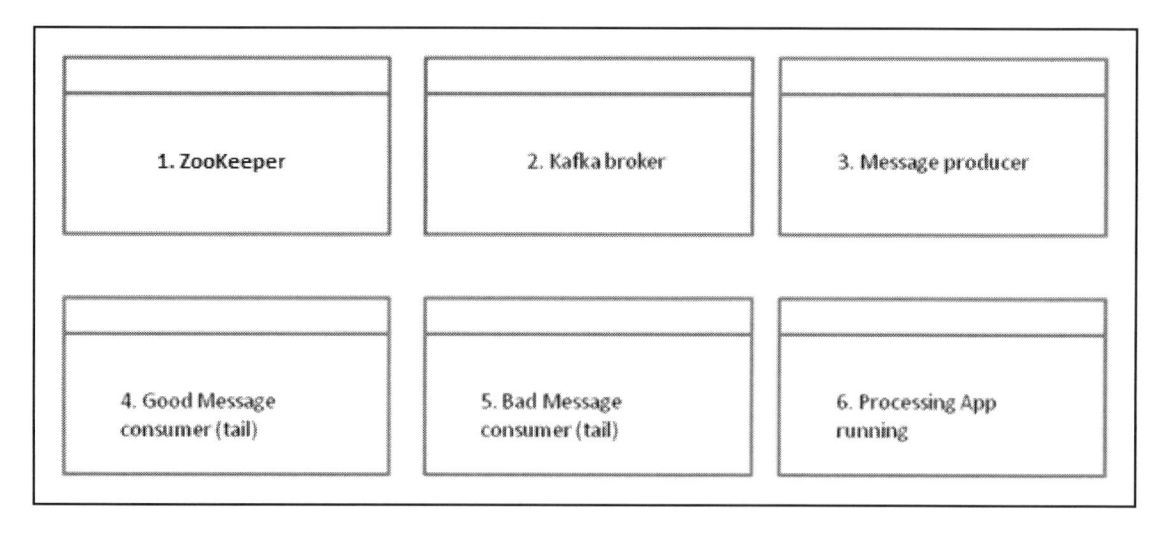

Figure 3.3: The six terminals to test the processing application including Zookeeper, Kafka broker, Message producer, Good Message consumer, Bad Message consumer, and the application itself

In the first command-line Terminal, this command is running in the Kafka directory:

```
$ bin/zookeeper-server-start.sh config/zookeeper.properties
```

In the second command-line Terminal, this command is running in the Kafka directory:

```
$ bin/kafka-server-start.sh config/server.properties
```

In the third command-line Terminal, go to the Kafka installation directory and generate the two necessary topics:

- `$ bin/kafka-topics.sh --create --zookeeper localhost:2181 --replication-factor 1 --partitions 1 --topic good-topic`
- `$ bin/kafka-topics.sh --create --zookeeper localhost:2181 --replication-factor 1 --partitions 1 --topic bad-topic`

Then, start the broker running the `source-topic` topic:

```
$ bin/kafka-console-producer.sh --broker-list localhost:9092 --topic source-topic
```

The preceding window is where the input messages are typed.

In the fourth command-line Terminal, start a consumer script listening to `good-topic`:

```
$ bin/kafka-console-consumer.sh --bootstrap-server localhost:9092 --from-beginning --topic good-topic
```

In the fifth command-line Terminal, start a consumer script listening to `bad-topic`:

```
$ bin/kafka-console-consumer.sh --bootstrap-server localhost:9092 --from-beginning --topic bad-topic
```

In the sixth command-line Terminal, start up the processing application. Go to the project root directory (where the Gradle `jar` command was executed) and run the following:

```
$ java -jar ./build/libs/doubloon-0.1.0.jar localhost:9092 vipConsumersGroup source-topic good-topic bad-topic
```

Go to the fourth command-line Terminal (the console producer) and send the following three messages (remember to press *Enter* between messages, and execute each one in just one line):

```
{"event": "CUSTOMER_SEES_BTCPRICE", "customer": {"id": "86689427", "name": "Edward S.", "ipAddress": "95.31.18.119"}, "currency": {"name": "bitcoin", "price": "USD"}, "timestamp": "2017-07-03T12:00:35Z"}

{"event": "CUSTOMER_SEES_BTCPRICE", "customer": {"id": "18313440", "name": "Julian A.", "ipAddress": "185.86.151.11"}, "currency": {"name": "bitcoin", "price": "USD"}, "timestamp": "2017-07-04T15:00:35Z"}

{"event": "CUSTOMER_SEES_BTCPRICE", "customer": {"id": "56886468", "name": "Lindsay M.", "ipAddress": "186.46.129.15"}, "currency": {"name": "bitcoin", "price": "USD"}, "timestamp": "2017-07-11T19:00:35Z"}
```

As these are cool messages, the messages typed in the console-producer should be appearing in the good-topic console-consumer window.

Now try sending bad messages. First, try messages that are not in JSON format:

```
I am not JSON, I am IT. [enter]
Hello! [enter]
```

This message should be received in the bad messages topic:

```
{"error": "JsonParseException: Unrecognized token ' I am not JSON, I am
IT.': was expecting 'null','true', 'false' or NaN
at [Source: I am not JSON, I am IT.; line: 1, column: 4]"}
```

Then try something more complex, such as the first message without a timestamp:

```
{"event": "CUSTOMER_SEES_BTCPRICE", "customer": {"id": "86689427", "name":
"Edward S.", "ipAddress": "95.31.18.119"}, "currency": {"name": "bitcoin",
"price": "USD"}}
```

This message should be received in the bad messages topic:

```
{"error": "timestamp is missing."}
```

There's more...

This recipe completes our validation. As one can see there is more validation to do, for example, validation against JSON schemas, but this is covered in subsequent chapters.

See also

- The validation architecture is detailed in the first diagram of this chapter and in the next chapter it will be enriched
- In the next chapter, the architecture of this chapter will be redesigned to incorporate message enrichment

4
Message Enrichment

In this chapter, we will cover the following recipes:

- Geolocation extractor
- Geolocation enricher
- Currency price extractor
- Currency price enricher
- Running the currency price enricher
- Modeling the events
- Setting up the project
- Open weather extractor
- Location temperature enricher
- Running the location temperature enricher

Introduction

The previous chapter focused on how to perform message validation with Kafka. This chapter is about message enrichment and the following chapter is about message composition. This chapter continues modeling the systems of Doubloon, the fictional company dedicated to cryptocurrency exchange.

Here, a new company is introduced, Treu Technologies. Treu is a fictional company dedicated to energy production and distribution. To operate, Treu uses a lot of **Internet of Things (IoT)** devices.

Treu also wants to implement an enterprise service bus with Apache Kafka. The goal is to manage all the messages received every minute from the machines and sensors. Treu has hundreds of machines sending thousands of messages per minute of different kinds to the enterprise service bus.

In the last chapter, the validation of the Doubloon messages was implemented. In this chapter we add enrichment. In this context, enriching means adding extra information to the messages. In the following recipes, the messages are enriched with the customer's geographical location using the geolocation database of MaxMind and a simple but effective example.

Each of the messages includes the IP address of the computer that our customer is using. To meet our business requirements, a company called MaxMind provides a free-to-use database that maps the IP addresses to geographical locations. In this context, the program looks up the customer's IP address in the MaxMind GeoIP database to determine where the customer is located at the point of the request. The use of algorithms or external sources to add extra data to a message is called enriching the messages.

Geolocation extractor

In Doubloon, there is a service that validates that the messages are well formed. But now, the business indicates that there should be validation at the customer's location. This is very simple, there is a term called a **bit license**, which limits virtual currency activities to a geographical area. At the time of writing, the regulations are limited to New York residents. For this purpose, those that reside, are located, have a place of business, or are conducting business, in the state of New York count as New York residents.

Getting ready

The execution of the recipes in `Chapter 3`, *Message Validation* is needed.

How to do it...

1. The first step is to open the `build.gradle` file on the Doubloon project created in `Chapter 3`, *Message Validation*, and add the lines in the following code:

    ```
    apply plugin: 'java'
    apply plugin: 'application'
    ```

```
sourceCompatibility = '1.8'

mainClassName = 'doubloon.ProcessingApp'

repositories {
  mavenCentral()
}

version = '0.2.0'

dependencies {
  compile 'org.apache.kafka:kafka-clients:0.11.0.1'
  compile 'com.maxmind.geoip:geoip-api:1.2.14'
  compile 'com.fasterxml.jackson.core:jackson-databind:2.6.3'
}

jar {
  manifest {
    attributes 'Main-Class': mainClassName
  }

  from {
    configurations.compile.collect {
      it.isDirectory() ? it : zipTree(it)
    }
  } {
    exclude "META-INF/*.SF"
    exclude "META-INF/*.DSA"
    exclude "META-INF/*.RSA"
  }
}
```

The first change is to switch from the 0.1.0 to the 0.2.0 version. The second change adds the MaxMind GeoIP API to the project.

2. To rebuild the app, from the project root directory run the following command:

    $ gradle jar

The output is something like the following:

    ```
    ...
    BUILD SUCCESSFUL
    Total time: 24.234 secs
    ```

3. The next step is to download a free copy of the MaxMind GeoIP database, with this command:

   ```
   $ wget
   "http://geolite.maxmind.com/download/geoip/database/GeoLiteCity.dat
   .gz"
   ```

4. To decompress the file, type this command:

   ```
   $ gunzip GeoLiteCity.dat.gz
   ```

   Put the `GeoLiteCity.dat` file in a location that can be accessed by our program

5. As the next step, create a file called `GeoIP.java` in the `src/main/java/doubloon/extractors` directory with the following contents:

   ```java
   package doubloon.extractors;

   import com.maxmind.geoip.Location;
   import com.maxmind.geoip.LookupService;
   import java.io.IOException;
   import java.util.logging.Level;
   import java.util.logging.Logger;

   public class GeoIP {

     private static final String MAXMINDDB = "/path to GeoLiteCity.dat file";

     public Location getLocation(String ipAddress) {
       try {
         LookupService maxmind = new LookupService(MAXMINDDB, LookupService.GEOIP_MEMORY_CACHE);
         Location location = maxmind.getLocation(ipAddress);
         return location;
       } catch (IOException ex) {
         Logger.getLogger(GeoIP.class.getName()).log(Level.SEVERE, null, ex);
       }

       return null;
     }

   }
   ```

How it works...

The `GeoIP` class has a public `getLocation` method that receives a string with the IP address and looks for that IP address in the GeoIP location database. The method returns a `Location` object with the geo-localization of that specific IP address.

There's more...

If for some reason downloading the database is not viable, MaxMind also exposes their services through an API. To read how to use this API, go to https://dev.maxmind.com/.

MaxMind also has interesting solutions to detect online fraud.

See also

- The MaxMind site: https://www.maxmind.com/
- To learn more about the bit license regulatory framework, visit: http://www.dfs.ny.gov/legal/regulations/bitlicense_reg_framework.htm

Geolocation enricher

Let's remember the Doubloon project requirements for the stream processing app. The *customer sees BTC price* event happens in the customer's web browser and is dispatched to Kafka via an HTTP event collector. The second step is to enrich the messages with the geolocation information. Remember from the previous chapter that defective messages result in bad data, so they are filtered.

Getting ready

Putting it all together, the specification is to create a stream application that does the following:

- Reads individual messages from a Kafka topic called **raw-messages**
- Validates the message, sending any invalid message to a dedicated Kafka topic called **invalid-messages**

Message Enrichment

- Enriches the message with the geolocation information
- Writes the enriched messages in a Kafka topic called **valid-messages**

All this is detailed in the following diagram and is the second version of the stream processing application:

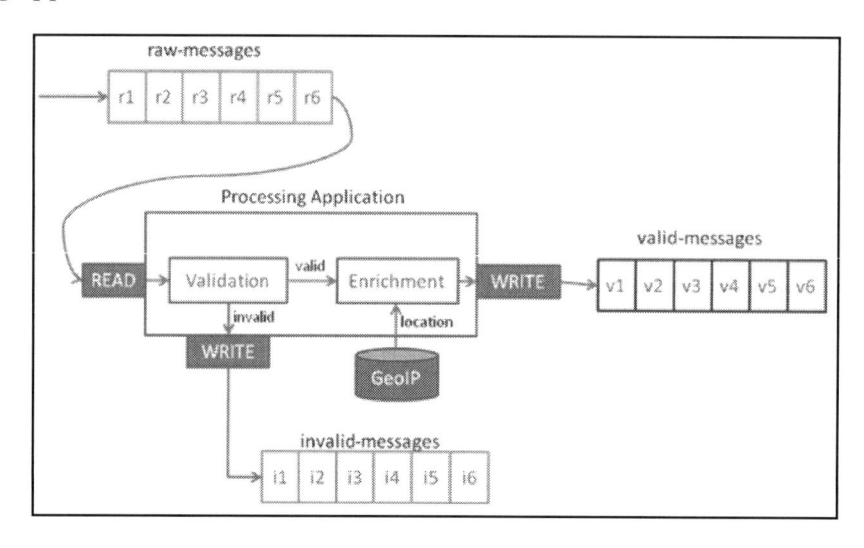

Figure 4.1: The processing application reads events from the raw-messages topic, validates the messages, routes the errors to the invalid-messages topic, enriches the messages with geolocation, and then writes them to the valid-messages topic

How to do it...

Create a file called `Enricher.java` in the `src/main/java/doubloon/` directory with the following contents:

```
package doubloon;

import com.fasterxml.jackson.databind.*;
import com.fasterxml.jackson.databind.node.ObjectNode;
import com.maxmind.geoip.Location;
import doubloon.extractors.GeoIP;

import java.io.IOException;

import org.apache.kafka.clients.producer.*;

public class Enricher implements Producer {
```

```
  private final KafkaProducer<String, String> producer;
  private final String goodTopic;
  private final String badTopic;

  protected static final ObjectMapper MAPPER = new ObjectMapper();

  public Enricher(String servers, String goodTopic,
        String badTopic) {
    this.producer = new KafkaProducer(
          Producer.createConfig(servers));
    this.goodTopic = goodTopic;
    this.badTopic = badTopic;
  }

  @Override
  public void process(String message) {

    try {
      JsonNode root = MAPPER.readTree(message);
      JsonNode ipAddressNode = root.path("customer").path("ipAddress");
      if (ipAddressNode.isMissingNode()) {
//1
        Producer.write(this.producer, this.badTopic,
              "{\"error\": \"customer.ipAddress is missing\"}");
      } else {
        String ipAddress = ipAddressNode.textValue();

        Location location = new GeoIP().getLocation(ipAddress);
//2
        ((ObjectNode) root).with("customer").put("country",
location.countryName);
//3
        ((ObjectNode) root).with("customer").put("city", location.city);
        Producer.write(this.producer, this.goodTopic,
              MAPPER.writeValueAsString(root));
//4
      }
    } catch (IOException e) {
      Producer.write(this.producer, this.badTopic, "{\"error\": \""
            + e.getClass().getSimpleName() + ": " + e.getMessage() +
"\"}");
    }
  }

}
```

Message Enrichment

How it works...

The `Enricher` implements the `Producer` interface. So, the `Enricher` is a Kafka producer.

- If the message does not have an IP address under customer, the message is automatically sent to the invalid-messages queue
- The `Enricher` calls the `getLocation` method of the `GeoIP` class
- The `country` and the `city` of the `Location` are added to the customer node
- The enriched message is written to the valid-messages topic

There's more...

Now we have our enricher, in the following recipes let's code the next version.

See also

- Note that the `Location` object has more information; in this example only the `country` and the `city` are extracted. But, what happens if more precision is required?
- Also note that here we have a very simple validation. Think about which validations are needed to warrant the correct operation of this system.

Currency price extractor

Okay, now in Doubloon there is a service that validates that the messages are well-formed. Also, the service enriches the messages with the customer's geolocation. Now the business indicates that they need a service that properly returns the requested currency price.

Getting ready

The execution of the previous recipes in this chapter is needed.

How to do it...

Go to the Open Exchange Rates page at: `https://openexchangerates.org/`. Register for a free plan to obtain your free API key. This key is needed to access the free API.

Create a file called `OpenExchange.java` in the `src/main/java/doubloon/extractors` directory with the following contents:

```
package doubloon.extractors;

import com.fasterxml.jackson.databind.JsonNode;
import com.fasterxml.jackson.databind.ObjectMapper;
import java.io.IOException;
import java.net.MalformedURLException;
import java.net.URL;
import java.util.logging.Level;
import java.util.logging.Logger;

public class OpenExchange {
  private static final String API_KEY = "API_KEY_VALUE";
//1
  protected static final ObjectMapper MAPPER = new ObjectMapper();
  public double getPrice(String currency) {
    try {
      URL url = new URL("https://openexchangerates.org/api/latest.json?app_id=" + API_KEY);
//2
      JsonNode root = MAPPER.readTree(url);
      JsonNode node = root.path("rates").path(currency);
//3
      return Double.parseDouble(node.toString());
//4
    } catch (MalformedURLException ex) {
      Logger.getLogger(OpenExchange.class.getName()).log(Level.SEVERE, null, ex);
    } catch (IOException ex) {
      Logger.getLogger(OpenExchange.class.getName()).log(Level.SEVERE, null, ex);
    }
    return 0;
  }
}
```

How it works...

The `OpenExchange` class has a public `getPrice` method that receives a string with the currency and returns the price in dollars for that currency. Specifically:

- To use the open exchange API, an API key is needed. Registration is free and gives 1,000 requests per month. Replace the code with your API key value.
- To check the prices of currencies at the moment, go to this URL: `https://openexchangerates.org/api/latest.json?app_id=YOUR_API_KEY`.
- The JSON returned by the URL is parsed looking for the specific currency.
- The requested price (in US dollars) is returned.

There's more...

Open Exchange Rates also expose their services through an API, to read how to use this API, go to: `https://docs.openexchangerates.org/`.

See also

- There are different ways to parse JSON, and there are entire books related to this topic. For this example, Jackson was used to parse JSON. To find more information, go to: `https://github.com/FasterXML`.
- Remember that this example uses the Open Exchange Rates free plan. If you need more precise or non-limited API requests, check the plans at: `https://openexchangerates.org/signup`.

Currency price enricher

The *customer sees BTC price* event happens in the customer's web browser and is dispatched to Kafka via an HTTP event collector. The second step is to enrich the messages with the geolocation information. The third step is to enrich the message with the currency price.

Getting ready

Recapitulating, the specification is to create a stream application that does the following:

- Reads individual messages from a Kafka topic called **raw-messages**
- Validates the messages, sending any invalid messages to a dedicated Kafka topic called **invalid-messages**
- Enriches the messages with the geolocation information and the currency price
- Writes the enriched messages in a Kafka topic called **valid-messages**

All this is detailed in the following diagram, which is the final version of the stream processing application:

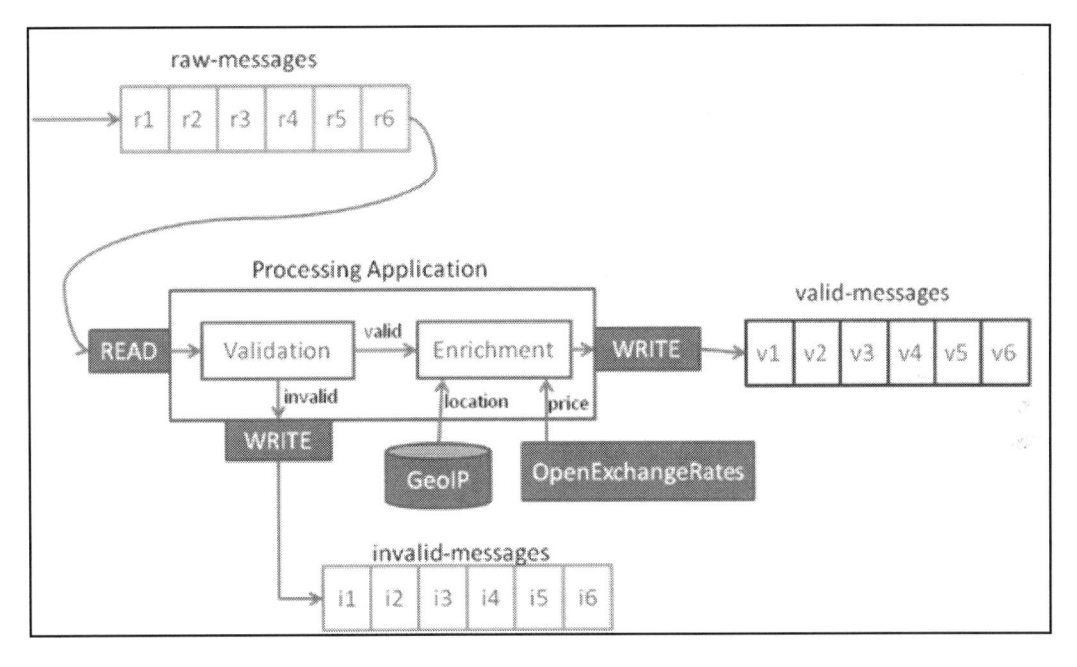

Figure 4.2: The processing application reads events from the raw-messages topic, validates the messages, routes the errors to the invalid-messages topic, enriches the messages with geolocation and prices, and finally, writes them to the valid-messages topic

Message Enrichment

How to do it...

Modify the `Enricher.java` file in the `src/main/java/doubloon/` directory with the following contents:

```
package doubloon;

import com.fasterxml.jackson.databind.*;
import com.fasterxml.jackson.databind.node.ObjectNode;
import com.maxmind.geoip.Location;
import doubloon.extractors.GeoIP;
import doubloon.extractors.OpenExchange;

import java.io.IOException;

import org.apache.kafka.clients.producer.*;

public class Enricher implements Producer {

  private final KafkaProducer<String, String> producer;
  private final String goodTopic;
  private final String badTopic;

  protected static final ObjectMapper MAPPER = new ObjectMapper();

  public Enricher(String servers, String goodTopic,
          String badTopic) {
    this.producer = new KafkaProducer(
            Producer.createConfig(servers));
    this.goodTopic = goodTopic;
    this.badTopic = badTopic;
  }

  @Override
  public void process(String message) {

    try {
      JsonNode root = MAPPER.readTree(message);
      JsonNode ipAddressNode = root.path("customer").path("ipAddress");
      if (ipAddressNode.isMissingNode()) {
//1
        Producer.write(this.producer, this.badTopic,
                "{\"error\": \"customer.ipAddress is missing\"}");
      } else {
        String ipAddress = ipAddressNode.textValue();

        Location location = new GeoIP().getLocation(ipAddress);
```

```
            ((ObjectNode) root).with("customer").put("country",
location.countryName);
            ((ObjectNode) root).with("customer").put("city", location.city);

            OpenExchange oe = new OpenExchange();
//2
            ((ObjectNode) root).with("currency").put("rate",
oe.getPrice("BTC"));
//3
            Producer.write(this.producer, this.goodTopic,
                MAPPER.writeValueAsString(root));
//4
        }
    } catch (IOException e) {
        Producer.write(this.producer, this.badTopic, "{\"error\": \""
            + e.getClass().getSimpleName() + ": " + e.getMessage() +
"\"}");
        }
    }
}
```

How it works...

The `Enricher` implements the `Producer` interface. So, the `Enricher` is a Kafka producer:

- If the message does not have an IP address under the customer, the message is automatically sent to the invalid-messages queue
- The `Enricher` generates an instance of the `OpenExchange` class as an extractor
- The `Enricher` calls the `getPrice` method of the `OpenExchange` class
- The `price` of the `currency` `BTC` is added to the `currency` node in the `price` leaf
- The enriched message is written to the valid-messages topic

There's more...

This is the final enricher for Doubloon. As can be seen, this pipeline architecture uses the extractors as input for the enrichers. The following recipe shows how to run the whole project.

See also

- Note that the JSON response has more information, for this example only the BTC price is used. The open data initiatives are free and provide a lot of free databases with online and historical data.

Running the currency price enricher

In the previous recipe, the final version of the `Enricher` class was coded. Now, in this recipe, everything is compiled and executed.

Getting ready

The execution of the previous recipes in this chapter is needed.

How to do it...

The `ProcessingApp` class coordinates the `Reader` and `Writer` classes. It contains the `main` method to execute them. Create a new file called `src/main/java/doubloon/ProcessingApp.java` and fill it with the following code:

```
package doubloon;

import java.io.IOException;

public class ProcessingApp {
  public static void main(String[] args) throws IOException{
    String servers = args[0];
    String groupId = args[1];
    String sourceTopic = args[2];
    String goodTopic = args[3];
    String badTopic = args[4];
    Reader reader = new Reader(servers, groupId, sourceTopic);
    Enricher enricher = new Enricher(servers, goodTopic, badTopic);
    reader.run(enricher);
  }
}
```

How it works...

The `ProcessingApp` receives five arguments from the command line:

- `args[0] servers`: This specifies the host and port of the Kafka broker
- `args[1] group id`: This specifies that the consumer belongs to this Kafka consumer group
- `args[2] source topic`: This is the topic that the reader will read from
- `args[3] good topic`: This is the topic where good messages will be sent
- `args[4] bad topic`: This the topic where bad messages will be sent

To build the project from the Doubloon directory, run the following command:

```
$ gradle jar
```

If everything is okay, the output should be as follows:

```
...
BUILD SUCCESSFUL
Total time: ...
```

To run the project, we have the six different command-line windows from the previous recipes. The following diagram shows how the arrangement of command-line windows should look:

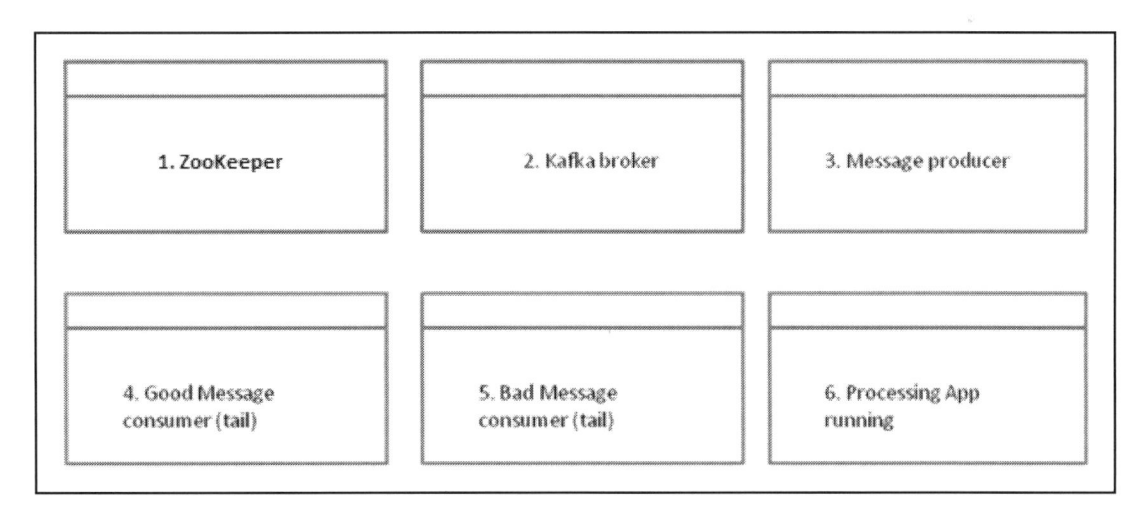

Figure 4.3: The six terminals to test the processing application including ZooKeeper, Kafka broker, Message producer, Good Message consumer, Bad Message consumer, and the application itself

Message Enrichment

In the first command-line Terminal, run ZooKeeper on the Kafka directory:

```
$ bin/zookeeper-server-start.sh config/zookeeper.properties
```

In the second command-line Terminal, run the broker on the Kafka directory:

```
$ bin/kafka-server-start.sh config/server.properties
```

In the third command-line Terminal, go to the Kafka installation directory and generate the two necessary topics:

- ```
  $ bin/kafka-topics.sh --create --zookeeper localhost:2181 --replication-factor 1 --partitions 1 --topic good-topic
  ```
- ```
  $ bin/kafka-topics.sh --create --zookeeper localhost:2181 --replication-factor 1 --partitions 1 --topic bad-topic
  ```

Then, start the broker running the `source-topic` topic:

```
$ bin/kafka-console-producer.sh --broker-list localhost:9092 --topic source-topic
```

This window is where the input messages are typed.

In the fourth command-line Terminal, start a consumer script listening to `good-topic`:

```
$ bin/kafka-console-consumer.sh --bootstrap-server localhost:9092 --from-beginning --topic good-topic
```

In the fifth command-line Terminal, start a consumer script listening to `bad-topic`:

```
$ bin/kafka-console-consumer.sh --bootstrap-server localhost:9092 --from-beginning --topic bad-topic
```

In the sixth command-line Terminal, start up the processing application. Go the project root directory (where the Gradle `jar` commands were executed) and run the following:

```
$ java -jar ./build/libs/doubloon-0.2.0.jar localhost:9092 vipConsumersGroup source-topic good-topic bad-topic
```

Go to the fourth command-line Terminal (the console-producer) and send the following three messages (remember to press enter between messages and execute each one in just one line):

```
{"event": "CUSTOMER_SEES_BTCPRICE", "customer": {"id": "86689427", "name": "Edward S.", "ipAddress": "95.31.18.119"}, "currency": {"name": "bitcoin", "price": "USD"}, "timestamp": "2017-07-03T12:00:35Z"}
```

```
{"event": "CUSTOMER_SEES_BTCPRICE", "customer": {"id": "18313440", "name":
"Julian A.", "ipAddress": "185.86.151.11"}, "currency": {"name": "bitcoin",
"price": "USD"}, "timestamp": "2017-07-04T15:00:35Z"}
```

As these are correct messages, the messages typed in the console-producer should be appearing enriched in the `good-topic` console-consumer window:

```
{"event":"CUSTOMER_SEES_BTCPRICE","customer":{"id":"86689427","name":"Edwar
d S.","ipAddress":"95.31.18.119","country":"Russian
Federation","city":"Moscow"},"currency":{"name":"bitcoin","price":"USD","ra
te":1.2132252E-4},"timestamp":"2017-07-03T12:00:35Z"}

{"event":"CUSTOMER_SEES_BTCPRICE","customer":{"id":"18313440","name":"Julia
n A.","ipAddress":"185.86.151.11","country":"United
Kingdom","city":"London"},"currency":{"name":"bitcoin","price":"USD","rate"
:1.2132252E-4},"timestamp":"2017-07-04T15:00:35Z"}

{"event":"CUSTOMER_SEES_BTCPRICE","customer":{"id":"56886468","name":"Linds
ay
M.","ipAddress":"186.46.129.15","country":"Ecuador","city":"Quito"},"curren
cy":{"name":"bitcoin","price":"USD","rate":1.2132252E-4},"timestamp":"2017-
07-11T19:00:35Z"}
```

Modeling the events

This recipe shows how to model the Treu messages in JSON format.

Getting ready

For this recipe, basic knowledge of JSON is required.

How to do it...

As mentioned, Treu Technologies has a lot of IoT machines that continuously send messages about their status to the control center.

These machines are used to generate electricity. So, it is very important for Treu to know the exact temperature of the machine and its state (running, shutdown, starting, shutting down, and so on).

Message Enrichment

Treu needs to know the weather forecast, because the machine should not operate over certain temperatures. These machines have different behaviors based on the temperature. It is different starting a machine in the cold than in warm conditions. The startup time also depends on the temperature. To warrant the electricity supply, the information has to be precise.

In a nutshell, it is always better to face an electrical power failure having to start the machines from warm than from cold.

The following code shows the representation of a machine status event in JSON:

```
{
    "event": "HEALTH_CHECK",
    "factory": "Hierve el agua, OAX",
    "serialNumber": " C3PO-R2D2",
    "type": "combined cycle",
    "status": "RUNNING",
    "lastStartedAt": 1511115511,
    "temperature": 34.56,
    "ipAddress": 192.168.210.11
}
```

How it works...

The proposed representation of this message in JSON has the following properties:

- `event`: This a string with the name of the message
- `factory`: This is the name of the factory where the machine is located
- `serialNumber`: This represents the machine serial number
- `type`: This represents the machine's type
- `status`: This a string that could be: `RUNNING`, `SHUT-DOWN`, `STARTING`, and `SHUTTING-DOWN`
- `lastStartedAt`: This is the time in Unix representation of the last start time
- `temperature`: This a double representing the machine's temperature in Celsius grades
- `ipAddress`: This is the machine's IP address

As one can see, this message can be read and understood by a human.

There's more...

To represent this message's schema, the template of all the messages of this type in Avro would be as follows:

```
{ "name": "health_check",
  "namespace": "treutec.avro",
  "type": "record",
  "fields": [
    { "name": "event", "type": "string" },
    { "name": "factory", "type": "string" },
    { "name": "serialNumber", "type": "string" },
    { "name": "type", "type": "string" },
    { "name": "status", "type": {
        "type": "enum", "symbols": ["STARTING", "RUNNING",
                                    "SHUTTING_DOWN", "SHUT-DOWN"] },
    { "name": "lastStartedAt", "type": "long",
      "logicalType": "timestamp-millis"},
    { "name": "temperature", "type": "float" },
    { "name": "ipAddress", "type": "string" }
    ]
}
```

See also

- For more information about schemas, check the Apache Avro specification at: http://avro.apache.org/docs/current/spec.html

Setting up the project

Before writing code, let's recall the project requirements for the Treu Technologies stream processing app.

Message Enrichment

Getting ready

Putting it all together, the specification is to create a stream application that does the following:

- Reads individual messages from a Kafka topic called **raw-messages**
- Enriches the messages with the geolocalization of the machine's IP address
- Enriches the messages with the weather information of the geolocalization
- Writes the correct events in a Kafka topic called **enriched-messages**

All these processes are detailed in the following diagram, which is the Treu stream processing application:

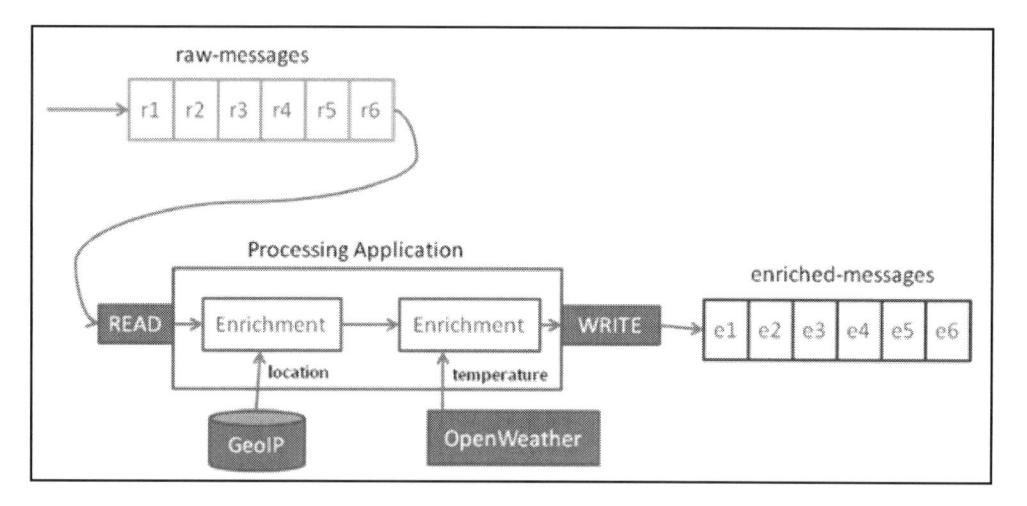

Figure 4.4: The processing application reads events from the raw-messages topic, enriches the messages with geolocalization and weather temperature information, and writes to the enriched-messages queue

How to do it...

1. The first step is to create our project with Gradle, which will be called `ProcessingApp`. Create a directory called `treu`, go to that directory, and execute the following:

    ```
    $ gradle init --type java-library
    ```

The output is something like the following:

```
...
BUILD SUCCESSFUL
...
```

2. Gradle creates a skeleton project in the directory, with two Java files called `Library.java` and `LibraryTest.java`. Feel free to delete both files. Your directory should be similar to the following:

```
- build.gradle
- gradle
-- wrapper
--- gradle-wrapper.jar
--- gradle-vreapper.properties
- gradlew
- gradle.bat
- settings.gradle
- src
-- main
--- java
----- Library.java
-- test
--- java
----- LibraryTest.java
```

3. Now, modify the `build.gradle` file and replace it with the following:

```
apply plugin: 'java'
apply plugin: 'application'

sourceCompatibility = '1.8'

mainClassName = 'treu.ProcessingApp'

repositories {
  mavenCentral()
}

version = '0.1.0'

dependencies {
  compile 'org.apache.kafka':'kafka-clients':0.11.0.1'
  compile 'com.maxmind.geoip:geoip-api:1.2.14'
  compile 'com.fasterxml.jackson.core:jackson-databind:2.6.3'
}
```

```
jar {
  manifest {
    attributes 'Main-Class': mainClassName
  }
  from {
    configurations.compile.collect {
      it.isDirectory() ? it : zipTree(it)
    }
  }
  {
  exclude "META-INF/*.SF"
  exclude "META-INF/*.DSA"
  exclude "META-INF/*.RSA"
}
}
```

How it works...

Some library dependencies were added to the application:

- `kafka_2.11`: These are the necessary dependencies for Apache Kafka
- `geoip-api1.2`: These are the necessary dependencies for MaxMind GeoIP
- `jackson-databind`: This is the library for JSON parsing and manipulation

To compile the sources and download the required libraries, type the following command:

```
$ gradle compileJava
```

The output should be as follows:

```
...
BUILD SUCCESSFUL
...
```

There's more...

The project can be created with Maven or SBT, even from the IDE. But for simplicity, here we created it with Gradle.

See also

- Gradle's main page: `http://www.gradle.org`
- Maven's main page: `http://maven.apache.org`
- SBT's main page: `http://www.scala-sbt.org/`

Open weather extractor

We have solved the problem of obtaining the geolocation from the IP address in this chapter. As the business requested, we also need to know the current temperature given a geolocation.

Getting ready

The execution of the previous recipe is needed.

How to do it...

Go to the OpenWeatherMap page at: `https://openweathermap.org/`. Register for a free plan to obtain your free API key, that key is needed to access the free API.

Create a file called `OpenWeather.java` in the `src/main/java/treu/extractors` directory with the following contents:

```
package treu.extractors;

import com.fasterxml.jackson.databind.JsonNode;
import com.fasterxml.jackson.databind.ObjectMapper;
import doubloon.extractors.OpenExchange;
import java.io.IOException;
import java.net.MalformedURLException;
import java.net.URL;
import java.util.logging.Level;
import java.util.logging.Logger;

public class OpenWeather {
  private static final String API_KEY = "API_KEY_VALUE";
//1
  protected static final ObjectMapper MAPPER = new ObjectMapper();
```

Message Enrichment

```
    public double getTemperature(String lat, String lon) {
      try {
        URL url = new
URL("http://api.openweathermap.org/data/2.5/weather?lat=" + lat + "&lon="+
lon + "&units=metric&appid=" + API_KEY);
        JsonNode root = MAPPER.readTree(url);
        JsonNode node = root.path("main").path("temp");
        return Double.parseDouble(node.toString());
      } catch (MalformedURLException ex) {
        Logger.getLogger(OpenExchange.class.getName()).log(Level.SEVERE,
null, ex);
      } catch (IOException ex) {
        Logger.getLogger(OpenExchange.class.getName()).log(Level.SEVERE,
null, ex);
      }
      return 0;
    }
}
```

How it works...

The `OpenWeather` class has a public `getTemperature` method that receives two string values with the latitude and longitude and returns the current temperature for those coordinates. Specifically:

- To use the `OpenWeather` API, an API key is needed, the registry is free and gives 1,000 requests per month. Replace the code with your API key value.
- To check the prices of the currencies at the moment, go to: `http://api.openweathermap.org/data/2.5/weather?lat=YOUR_LATlon=YOUR_LONGunits=metricappid=YOUR_API_KEY`.
- The JSON returned by the URL is parsed looking for the temperature.
- The requested temperature (in degrees Celsius) is returned.

There's more...

OpenWeatherMap also exposes their services through an API, to read how to use this API go to: `https://openweathermap.org/api`.

See also

- There are different ways to parse JSON, and there are entire books related to this topic. For this example, Jackson was used to parse the JSON, to find more information go to: https://github.com/FasterXML.

Location temperature enricher

The next step is to enrich the messages with the geolocation information. The third step is to enrich the message with the temperature.

Getting ready

Recapitulating, the specification is to create a stream application that does the following:

- Reads individual messages from a Kafka topic called **raw-messages**
- Enriches the messages with the geolocalization of the machine's IP address
- Enriches the messages with the weather information of the geolocalization
- Writes the correct events in a Kafka topic called **enriched-messages**

How to do it...

Modify the `Enricher.java` file in the `src/main/java/treu/` directory with the following contents:

```
package treu;

import com.fasterxml.jackson.databind.*;
import com.fasterxml.jackson.databind.node.ObjectNode;
import com.maxmind.geoip.Location;
import treu.extractors.GeoIP;
import treu.extractors.OpenWeather;

import java.io.IOException;

import org.apache.kafka.clients.producer.*;

public class Enricher implements Producer {
```

Message Enrichment

```
    private final KafkaProducer<String, String> producer;
    private final String enrichedTopic;

    protected static final ObjectMapper MAPPER = new ObjectMapper();

    public Enricher(String servers, String enrichedTopic) {
      this.producer = new KafkaProducer(Producer.createConfig(servers));
      this.enrichedTopic = enrichedTopic;
    }

    @Override
    public void process(String message) {

      try {
        JsonNode root = MAPPER.readTree(message);
        JsonNode ipAddressNode = root.path("ipAddress");
        if (!ipAddressNode.isMissingNode()) {
          String ipAddress = ipAddressNode.textValue();

          Location location = new GeoIP().getLocation(ipAddress);
//1

          OpenWeather ow = new OpenWeather();
//2
          ((ObjectNode) root).with("location").put("temperature",
                  ow.getTemperature(location.latitude + "",
                                    location.longitude + ""));
//3
          Producer.write(this.producer, this.enrichedTopic,
                  MAPPER.writeValueAsString(root));
//4
        }
      } catch (IOException e) {
        // deal with exception
      }
    }

}
```

How it works...

The `Enricher` implements the `Producer` interface. So, the `Enricher` is a Kafka producer:

- The `Enricher` generates an instance of the `GeoIP` class and obtains the location based on the IP address
- The `Enricher` generates an instance of the `OpenWeather` class and obtains the temperature based on the location
- The `Enricher` calls the `getTemperature` method of the `OpenWeather` class
- The `temperature` of the location is added to the `location` node in the `temperature` leaf

There's more...

This is the final enricher for Treu. As can be seen, this pipeline architecture uses the extractors as input for the enrichers. The following recipe shows how to run the project.

See also

- Note that both JSON responses have so much more information. OpenWeatherMap has more historical information and forecasts about the weather.

Running the location temperature enricher

In the previous recipe, the final version of the `Enricher` class was coded. Now, in this recipe, everything is compiled and executed.

Getting ready

The execution of the previous recipe in this chapter is needed.

Message Enrichment

How to do it...

The `ProcessingApp` class coordinates the `Reader` and `Writer` classes. It contains the `main` method to execute them. Create a new file called `src/main/java/treu/ProcessingApp.java` and fill it with the following code:

```
package treu;

import java.io.IOException;

public class ProcessingApp {

  public static void main(String[] args) throws IOException{
    String servers = args[0];
    String groupId = args[1];
    String sourceTopic = args[2];
    String enrichedTopic = args[3];
    Reader reader = new Reader(servers, groupId, sourceTopic);
    Enricher enricher = new Enricher(servers, goodTopic, enrichedTopic);
    reader.run(enricher);
  }
}
```

How it works...

The `ProcessingApp` receives four arguments from the command line:

- `args[0] servers`: This specifies the host and port of the Kafka broker
- `args[1] group id`: This specifies that the consumer belongs to this Kafka consumer group
- `args[2] source topic`: This is the topic the reader will read from
- `args[3] good topic`: This is the topic where enriched messages will be sent

To build the project from the `treu` directory, run the following command:

```
$ gradle jar
```

If everything is okay, the output should be as follows:

```
...
BUILD SUCCESSFUL
Total time: ...
```

To run the project, we have the five different command-line windows from the previous recipes. The following diagram shows how the arrangement of command-line windows should look:

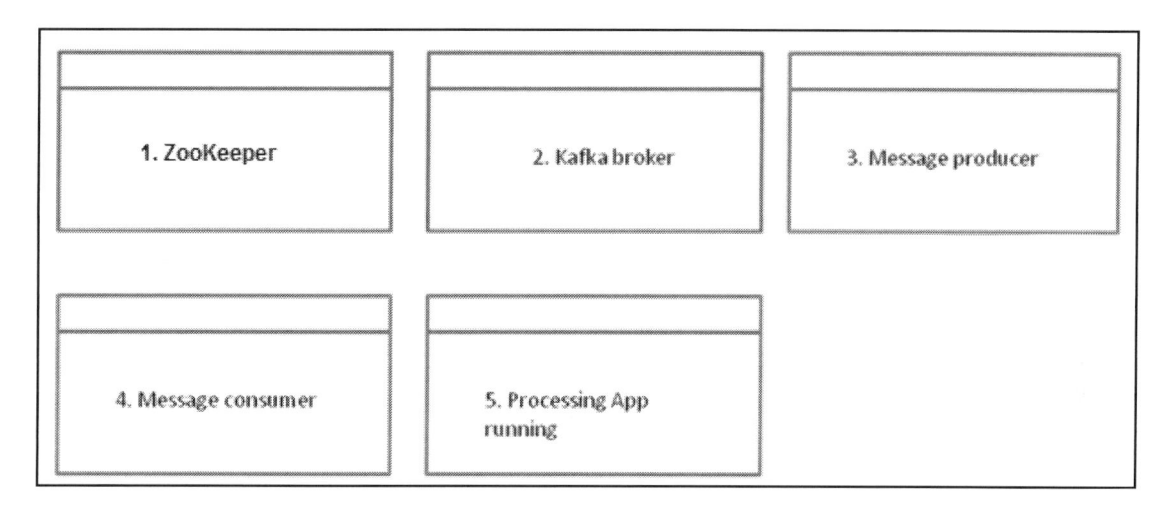

Figure 4.5: The five terminals to test the processing application including ZooKeeper, Kafka broker, Message producer, Message consumer, and the application itself

In the first command-line Terminal, start ZooKeeper in the Kafka directory:

```
$ bin/zookeeper-server-start.sh config/zookeeper.properties
```

In the second command-line Terminal, start the broker in the Kafka directory:

```
$ bin/kafka-server-start.sh config/server.properties
```

In the third command-line Terminal, go to the Kafka installation directory and generate the two necessary topics:

- `$ bin/kafka-topics.sh --create --zookeeper localhost:2181 --replication-factor 1 --partitions 1 --topic raw-messages`
- `$ bin/kafka-topics.sh --create --zookeeper localhost:2181 --replication-factor 1 --partitions 1 --topic enriched-messages`

Then, start the broker running the `raw-messages` topic:

```
$ bin/kafka-console-producer.sh --broker-list localhost:9092 --topic raw-messages
```

Message Enrichment

This window is where the input messages are typed.

In the fourth command-line Terminal, start a consumer script listening to `enriched-messages`:

```
$ bin/kafka-console-consumer.sh --bootstrap-server localhost:9092 --from-beginning --topic enriched-messages
```

In the fifth command-line Terminal, start up the processing application. Go the project root directory (where the Gradle `jar` commands were executed) and run:

```
$ java -jar ./build/libs/treu-0.1.0.jar localhost:9092 vipConsumersGroup raw-messages enriched-messages
```

Go to the third command-line Terminal (the console-producer) and send the following message (remember to execute it in just one line):

```
{
    "event": "HEALTH_CHECK",
    "factory": "Hierve el agua, OAX",
    "serialNumber": " C3PO-R2D2",
    "type": "combined cycle",
    "status": "RUNNING",
    "lastStartedAt": 1511115511,
    "temperature": 34.56,
    "ipAddress": 192.168.210.11
}
```

As this is a well-formed message, the messages typed in the console-producer should be appearing enriched in the `enriched-messages` console-consumer window:

```
{
    "event": "HEALTH_CHECK",
    "factory": "Hierve el agua, OAX",
    "serialNumber": " C3PO-R2D2",
    "type": "combined cycle",
    "status": "RUNNING",
    "lastStartedAt": 1511115511,
    "temperature": 34.56,
    "ipAddress": 192.168.210.11,
    "location": {
        "temperature": 20.12
    }
}
```

5
The Confluent Platform

This chapter covers the following recipes:

- Installing the Confluent Platform
- Using Kafka operations
- Monitoring with the Confluent Control Center
- Using the Schema Registry
- Using the Kafka REST Proxy
- Using Kafka Connect

Introduction

The Confluent Platform is a full stream data system. It enables you to organize and manage data from several sources in one high-performance and reliable system. As mentioned in the first few chapters, the goal of an enterprise service bus is not only to provide the system a means to transport messages and data but also to provide all the tools that are required to connect the data origins (data sources), applications, and data destinations (data sinks) to the platform.

The Confluent Platform has these parts:

- Confluent Platform open source
- Confluent Platform enterprise
- Confluent Cloud

The Confluent Platform

The Confluent Platform open source has the following components:

- Apache Kafka core
- Kafka Streams
- Kafka Connect
- Kafka clients
- Kafka REST Proxy
- Kafka Schema Registry

The Confluent Platform enterprise has the following components:

- Confluent Control Center
- Confluent support, professional services, and consulting

All the components are open source except the Confluent Control Center, which is a proprietary of Confluent Inc.

An explanation of each component is as follows:

- **Kafka core**: The Kafka brokers discussed at the moment in this book.
- **Kafka Streams**: The Kafka library used to build stream processing systems.
- **Kafka Connect**: The framework used to connect Kafka with databases, stores, and filesystems.
- **Kafka clients**: The libraries for writing/reading messages to/from Kafka. Note that there clients for these languages: Java, Scala, C/C++, Python, and Go.
- **Kafka REST Proxy**: If the application doesn't run in the Kafka clients' programming languages, this proxy allows connecting to Kafka through HTTP.
- **Kafka Schema Registry**: Recall that an enterprise service bus should have a message template repository. The Schema Registry is the repository of all the schemas and their historical versions, made to ensure that if an endpoint changes, then all the involved parts are acknowledged.
- **Confluent Control Center**: A powerful web graphic user interface for managing and monitoring Kafka systems.
- **Confluent Cloud**: Kafka as a service—a cloud service to reduce the burden of operations.

Installing the Confluent Platform

In order to use the REST proxy and the Schema Registry, we need to install the Confluent Platform. Also, the Confluent Platform has important administration, operation, and monitoring features fundamental for modern Kafka production systems.

Getting ready

At the time of writing this book, the Confluent Platform Version is 4.0.0.

Currently, the supported operating systems are:

- Debian 8
- Red Hat Enterprise Linux
- CentOS 6.8 or 7.2
- Ubuntu 14.04 LTS and 16.04 LTS

macOS currently is just supported for testing and development purposes, not for production environments. Windows is not yet supported. Oracle Java 1.7 or higher is required.

The default ports for the components are:

- `2181`: Apache ZooKeeper
- `8081`: Schema Registry (REST API)
- `8082`: Kafka REST Proxy
- `8083`: Kafka Connect (REST API)
- `9021`: Confluent Control Center
- `9092`: Apache Kafka brokers

It is important to have these ports, or the ports where the components are going to run, open.

How to do it...

There are two ways to install: downloading the compressed files or with `apt-get` command.

To install the compressed files:

1. Download the Confluent open source v4.0 or Confluent Enterprise v4.0 TAR files from https://www.confluent.io/download/
2. Uncompress the archive file (the recommended path for installation is under `/opt`)
3. To start the Confluent Platform, run this command:

   ```
   $ <confluent-path>/bin/confluent start
   ```

   The output should be as follows:

   ```
   Starting zookeeper
   zookeeper is [UP]
   Starting kafka
   kafka is [UP]
   Starting schema-registry
   schema-registry is [UP]
   Starting kafka-rest
   kafka-rest is [UP]
   Starting connect
   connect is [UP]
   ```

To install with the `apt-get` command (in Debian and Ubuntu):

1. Install the Confluent public key used to sign the packages in the APT repository:

   ```
   $ wget -qO - http://packages.confluent.io/deb/4.0/archive.key | sudo apt-key add -
   ```

2. Add the repository to the sources list:

   ```
   $ sudo add-apt-repository "deb [arch=amd64] http://packages.confluent.io/deb/4.0 stable main"
   ```

3. Finally, run the `apt-get` update to install the Confluent Platform
4. To install Confluent open source:

   ```
   $ sudo apt-get update && sudo apt-get install confluent-platform-oss-2.11
   ```

5. To install Confluent Enterprise:

   ```
   $ sudo apt-get update && sudo apt-get install confluent-platform-2.11
   ```

   > The end of the package name specifies the Scala version. Currently, the supported versions are 2.11 (recommended) and 2.10.

There's more...

The Confluent Platform provides the system and component packages. The commands in this recipe are for installing all components of the platform. To install individual components, follow the instructions on this page: https://docs.confluent.io/current/installation/available_packages.html#available-packages.

See also

- In modern environments, the Confluent Platform can also be installed using Docker images; for more information, visit the following link: https://docs.confluent.io/current/installation/docker/docs/index.html#cpdocker-intro.

Using Kafka operations

With the Confluent Platform installed, the administration, operation, and monitoring of Kafka become very simple. Let's review how to operate Kafka with the Confluent Platform.

Getting ready

For this recipe, Confluent should be installed, up, and running.

How to do it...

The commands in this section should be executed from the directory where the Confluent Platform is installed:

1. To start ZooKeeper, Kafka, and the Schema Registry with one command, run:

   ```
   $ confluent start schema-registry
   ```

   The output of this command should be:

   ```
   Starting zookeeper
   zookeeper is [UP]
   Starting kafka
   kafka is [UP]
   Starting schema-registry
   schema-registry is [UP]
   ```

   > **TIP:** To execute the commands outside the installation directory, add Confluent's `bin` directory to `PATH`:
   > `export PATH=<path_to_confluent>/bin:$PATH`

2. To manually start each service with its own command, run:

   ```
   $ ./bin/zookeeper-server-start ./etc/kafka/zookeeper.properties
   $ ./bin/kafka-server-start ./etc/kafka/server.properties
   $ ./bin/schema-registry-start ./etc/schema-registry/schema-registry.properties
   ```

   Note that the syntax of all the commands is exactly the same as always but without the `.sh` extension.

3. To create a topic called `test_topic`, run the following command:

   ```
   $ ./bin/kafka-topics --zookeeper localhost:2181 --create --topic test_topic --partitions 1 --replication-factor 1
   ```

4. To send an Avro message to `test_topic` in the broker without writing a single line of code, use the following command:

   ```
   $ ./bin/kafka-avro-console-producer --broker-list localhost:9092
       --topic test_topic --property
   value.schema='{"name":"person","type":"record",
   "fields":[{"name":"name","type":"string"},{"name":"age","type":"int
   "}]}'
   ```

5. Send some messages and press *Enter* after each line:

   ```
   {"name": "Alice", "age": 27}
   {"name": "Bob", "age": 30}
   {"name": "Charles", "age":57}
   ```

6. *Enter* with an empty line is interpreted as null. To shut down the process, press *Ctrl + C*.

7. To consume the Avro messages from `test_topic` since the beginning, type:

   ```
   $ ./bin/kafka-avro-console-consumer --topic test_topic --zookeeper localhost:2181 --from-beginning
   ```

   The messages created in the previous step will be written to the console in the format they were introduced.

8. To shut down the consumer, press *Ctrl + C*.

9. To test the Avro schema validation, try to produce data on the same topic using an incompatible schema, for example, with this producer:

   ```
   $ ./bin/kafka-avro-console-producer --broker-list localhost:9092
       --topic test_topic --property value.schema='{"type":"string"}'
   ```

10. After you've hit *Enter* on the first message, the following exception is raised:

    ```
    org.apache.kafka.common.errors.SerializationException: Error registering Avro schema: "string"
    Caused by:
    io.confluent.kafka.schemaregistry.client.rest.exceptions.RestClientException: Schema being registered is incompatible with the latest schema; error code: 409
            at
    io.confluent.kafka.schemaregistry.client.rest.utils.RestUtils.httpRequest(RestUtils.java:146)
    ```

11. To shut down the services (Schema Registry, broker, and ZooKeeper) run:

    ```
    confluent stop
    ```

12. To delete all the producer messages stored in the broker, run this:

    ```
    confluent destroy
    ```

There's more...

With the Confluent Platform, it is possible to manage all of the Kafka system through the Kafka operations, which are classified as follows:

- **Production deployment**: Hardware configuration, file descriptors, and ZooKeeper configuration
- **Post deployment**: Admin operations, rolling restart, backup, and restoration
- **Auto data balancing**: Rebalancer execution and decommissioning brokers
- **Monitoring**: Metrics for each concept—broker, ZooKeeper, topics, producers, and consumers
- **Metrics reporter**: Message size, security, authentication, authorization, and verification

See also

- To see the complete list of Kafka operations available, check out this URL: `https://docs.confluent.io/current/kafka/operations.html`

Monitoring with the Confluent Control Center

This recipe shows you how to use the metrics reporter of the Confluent Control Center.

Getting ready

The execution of the previous recipe is needed.

Before starting the Control Center, configure the metrics reporter:

1. Back up the `server.properties` file located at:

    `<confluent_path>/etc/kafka/server.properties`

2. In the `server.properties` file, uncomment the following lines:

   ```
   metric.reporters=io.confluent.metrics.reporter.ConfluentMetricsReporter
   confluent.metrics.reporter.bootstrap.servers=localhost:9092
   confluent.metrics.reporter.topic.replicas=1
   ```

3. Back up the Kafka Connect configuration located in:

   `<confluent_path>/etc/schema-registry/connect-avro-distributed.properties`

4. Add the following lines at the end of the `connect-avro-distributed.properties` file:

   ```
   consumer.interceptor.classes=io.confluent.monitoring.clients.interceptor.MonitoringConsumerInterceptor
   producer.interceptor.classes=io.confluent.monitoring.clients.interceptor.MonitoringProducerInterceptor
   ```

5. Start the Confluent Platform:

   `$ <confluent_path>/bin/confluent start`

Before starting the Control Center, change its configuration:

6. Back up the `control-center.properties` file located in:

   `<confluent_path>/etc/confluent-control-center/control-center.properties`

7. Add the following lines at the end of the `control-center.properties` file:

   ```
   confluent.controlcenter.internal.topics.partitions=1
   confluent.controlcenter.internal.topics.replication=1
   confluent.controlcenter.command.topic.replication=1
   confluent.monitoring.interceptor.topic.partitions=1
   confluent.monitoring.interceptor.topic.replication=1
   confluent.metrics.topic.partitions=1
   confluent.metrics.topic.replication=1
   ```

8. Start the Control Center:

   `<confluent_path>/bin/control-center-start`

How to do it...

1. Open the Control Center web graphic user interface at the following URL: `http://localhost:9021/`.

2. The `test_topic` created in the previous recipe is needed:

   ```
   $ <confluent_path>/bin/kafka-topics --zookeeper localhost:2181 --create --test_topic --partitions 1 --replication-factor 1
   ```

3. From the Control Center, click on the **Kafka Connect** button on the left. Click on the **New source** button:

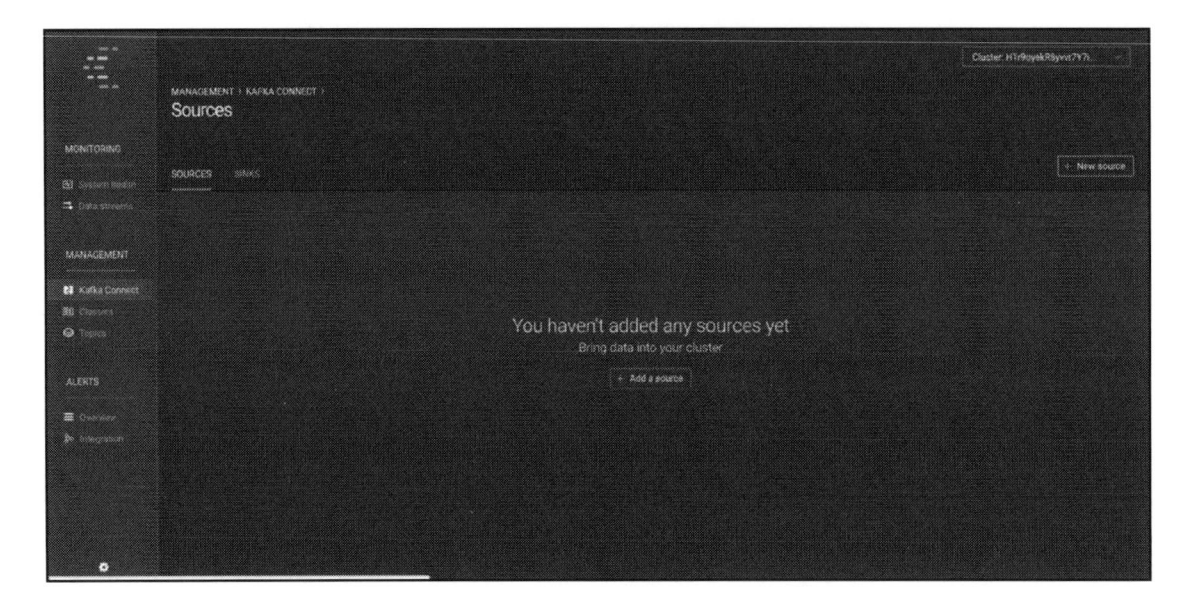

4. From the connector class, drop down the menu and select `SchemaSourceConnector`. Specify **Connection Name** as `Schema-Avro-Source`.

5. In the topic name, specify `test_topic`.

6. Click on **Continue**, and then click on the **Save & Finish** button to apply the configuration.

To create a new sink follow these steps:

1. From Kafka Connect, click on the **SINKS** button and then on the **New sink** button:

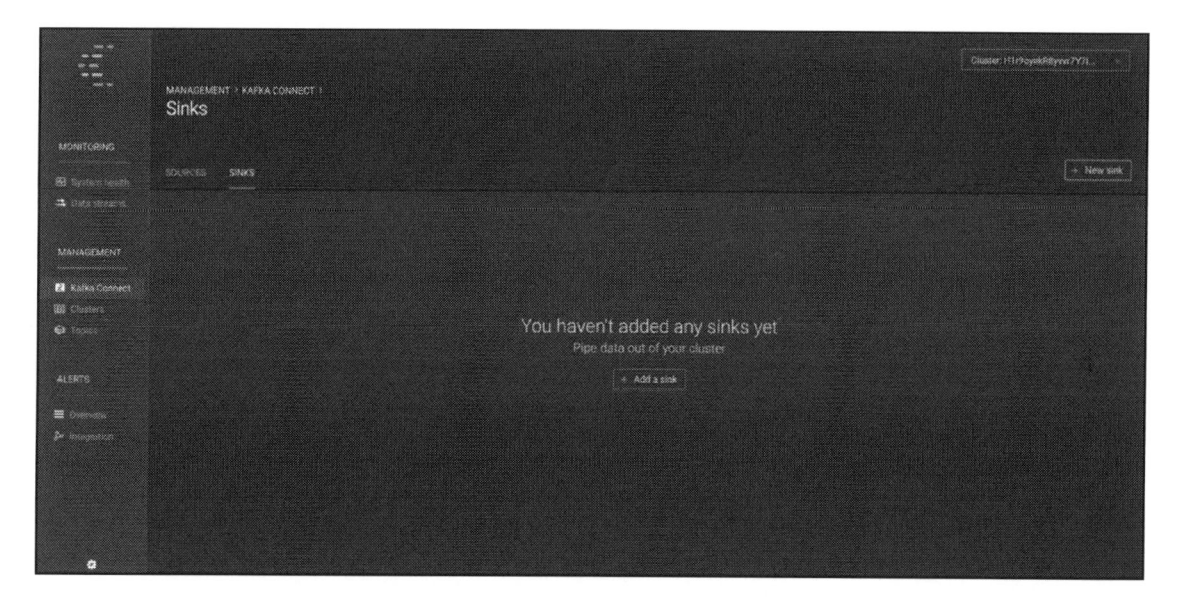

2. From the topics list, choose `test_topic` and click on the **Continue** button
3. In the **SINKS** tab, set the connection class to `SchemaSourceConnector`; specify **Connection Name** as `Schema-Avro-Source`
4. Click on the **Continue** button and then on **Save & Finish** to apply the new configuration

The Confluent Platform

How it works...
Click on the **Data streams** tab and a chart shows the total number of messages produced and consumed on the cluster:

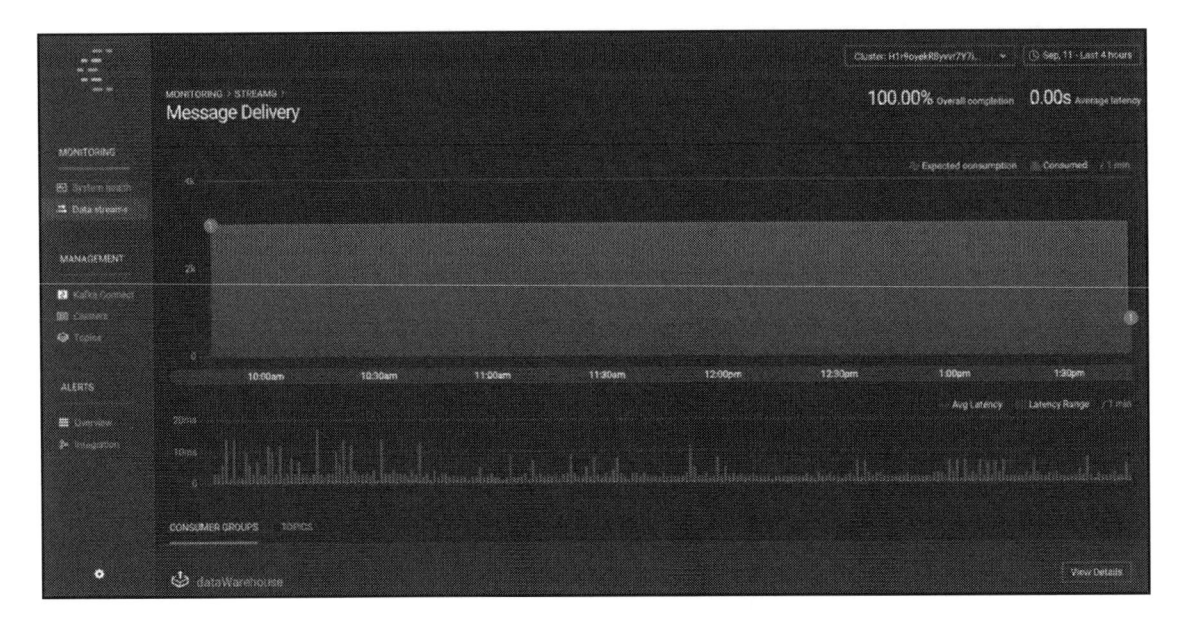

There's more...
To see the full documentation of the Control Center monitoring Kafka, visit this URL: `https://docs.confluent.io/current/kafka/monitoring.html`.

Using the Schema Registry
The Schema Registry is a repository. It is a metadata-serving layer for schemas. It provides a REST interface for storing and retrieving Avro schemas. It has a versioned history of schemas and provides compatibility analysis to leverage schema evolution based on that compatibility.

Remember that the Schema Registry has a REST interface; so, in this recipe, we use Java to make HTTP requests, but it is precisely a REST interface used to promote language and platform neutrality.

Getting ready

The Confluent Platform should be up and running:

```
$ confluent start schema-registry
```

How to do it...

Remember the *Customer sees BTC price* Avro schema of Doubloon:

```
{ "name": "customer_sees_btcprice",
  "namespace": "doubloon.avro",
  "type": "record",
  "fields": [
    { "name": "event", "type": "string" },
    { "name": "customer",
      "type": {
         "name": "id", "type": "long",
         "name": "name", "type": "string",
         "name": "ipAddress", "type": "string"
      }
    },
    { "name": "currency",
      "type": {
         "name": "name", "type": "string",
         "name": "price", "type": {
         "type": "enum", "namespace": "doubloon.avro",
            "name": "priceEnum", "symbols": ["USD", "EUR"]}
      }
    },
    { "name": "timestamp", "type": "long",
      "logicalType": "timestamp-millis"
    }
  ]
}
```

The Confluent Platform

Let's use the Schema Registry from Java:

1. Store the content of the Avro schema in a `String` variable:

   ```
   String CSBP_SCHEMA = " "{n" + ""schema": "" + .../*content here*/ +
   "}";
   ```

2. To interact with HTTP, this example uses the `okhttp3` Java library:

   ```
   import okhttp3.*;
   ...
   ```

3. Declare this variable:

   ```
   OkHttpClient client = new OkHttpClient();
   ```

4. To manipulate the content type schemas, declare this variable:

   ```
   private final static MediaType SCHEMA_CONTENT =
   MediaType.parse("application/vnd.schemaregistry.v1+json");
   ```

5. This is an equivalent of the following in HTTP:

   ```
   "Content-Type: application/vnd.schemaregistry.v1+json"
   ```

6. To post (add) this new schema to the Schema Registry:

   ```
   Request request = new Request.Builder()
           .post(RequestBody.create(SCHEMA_CONTENT, CSBP_SCHEMA))
           .url("http://localhost:8081/subjects/CSBP/versions")
           .build();

   String output = client.newCall(request).execute().body().string();
   ```

7. To list all the schemas stored in the Schema Registry:

   ```
   request = new Request.Builder()
              .url("http://localhost:8081/subjects")
              .build();

   output = client.newCall(request).execute().body().string();
   ```

8. To display all versions of the CSBP schema:

   ```
   request = new Request.Builder()
               .url("http://localhost:8081/subjects/CSBP/versions/")
               .build();

   output = client.newCall(request).execute().body().string();
   ```

9. To display version 2 of the CSBP schema:

   ```
   request = new Request.Builder()
               .url("http://localhost:8081/subjects/CSBP/versions/2")
               .build();

   output = client.newCall(request).execute().body().string();
   ```

10. To display the schema with ID 5:

    ```
    request = new Request.Builder()
                .url("http://localhost:8081/schemas/ids/5")
                .build();

    output = client.newCall(request).execute().body().string();
    ```

11. To display the latest version of CSBP:

    ```
    request = new Request.Builder()
    .url("http://localhost:8081/subjects/CSBP/versions/latest")
                .build();

    output = client.newCall(request).execute().body().string();
    ```

12. To check whether a schema is registered:

    ```
    request = new Request.Builder()
                .post(RequestBody.create(SCHEMA_CONTENT, CSBP_SCHEMA))
                .url("http://localhost:8081/subjects/CSBP")
                .build();

    output = client.newCall(request).execute().body().string();
    ```

13. To test the schema compatibility:

    ```
    request = new Request.Builder()
                .post(RequestBody.create(SCHEMA_CONTENT,
    CSBP_SCHEMA))
    .url("http://localhost:8081/compatibility/subjects/CSBP/versions/latest")
                .build();

    output = client.newCall(request).execute().body().string();
    ```

14. To display the top-level compatibility:

    ```
    request = new Request.Builder()
                .url("http://localhost:8081/config")
                .build();

    output = client.newCall(request).execute().body().string();
    ```

15. To set a top-level compatibility configuration, the possible values are none, backward, forward, and full:

    ```
    request = new Request.Builder()
                .put(RequestBody.create(SCHEMA_CONTENT,
    "{"compatibility": "none"}"))
                .url("http://localhost:8081/config")
                .build();

    output = client.newCall(request).execute().body().string();
    ```

16. To set the compatibility configuration for CSBP, the possible values are none, backward, forward, and full:

    ```
    request = new Request.Builder()
                .put(RequestBody.create(SCHEMA_CONTENT,
    "{"compatibility": "backward"}"))
                .url("http://localhost:8081/config/CSBP")
                .build();

    output = client.newCall(request).execute().body().string();
    ```

See also

- To see the full documentation of the Schema Registry, visit this URL: `https://docs.confluent.io/current/schema-registry/docs/index.html`

Using the Kafka REST Proxy

What happens if we want to use Kafka in an environment that is not yet supported? Think in terms of something such as JavaScript, PHP, and so on.

For this and other programming challenges, the Kafka REST Proxy provides a RESTful interface to a Kafka cluster.

From a REST interface, one can produce and consume messages, view the state of the cluster, and perform administrative actions without using the native Kafka protocol or clients.

The example use cases are:

- Sending data to Kafka from a frontend app built in a non-supported language (yes, think of the JavaScript and PHP fronts, for example).
- The need to communicate with Kafka from an environment that doesn't support Kafka (think in terms of mainframes and legacy systems).
- Scripting administrative actions. Think of a DevOps team in charge of a Kafka system and a sysadmin who doesn't know the supported languages (Java, Scala, Python, Go, or C/C++).

Getting ready

The Confluent Platform should be up and running:

```
$ confluent start kafka-rest
```

How to do it...

The examples in this recipe are written using the `curl` command to empathize language and platform independence. It could have been coded in JavaScript and PHP, but neutrality is empathized.

1. To send the `{"employee":1234}` JSON message to the `open_topic` topic:

    ```
    $ curl -X POST -H "Content-Type: application/vnd.kafka.json.v2+json"
          -H "Accept: application/vnd.kafka.v2+json"
          --data '{"records":[{"value":{"employee":1234}}]}'
    "http://localhost:8082/topics/open_topic"
    {"offsets":[{"partition":0,"offset":0,"error_code":null,"error":null}],"key_schema_id":null,"value_schema_id":null}
    ```

2. To create a consumer for JSON data:

    ```
    $ curl -X POST -H "Content-Type: application/vnd.kafka.v2+json"
          --data '{"name": "powerful_consumer_instance", "format": "json", "auto.offset.reset": "earliest"}'
          http://localhost:8082/consumers/powerful_json_consumer
      {"instance_id":"powerful_consumer_instance",
    "base_uri":"http://localhost:8082/consumers/powerful_json_consumer/instances/powerful_consumer_instance"}
    ```

3. To subscribe `powerful_consumer` to the `open_topic` topic:

    ```
    $ curl -X POST -H "Content-Type: application/vnd.kafka.v2+json" --data '{"topics":["open_topic"]}'
    http://localhost:8082/consumers/powerful_json_consumer/instances/powerful_consumer_instance/subscription
    ```

    There is no content in the response.

4. To consume some data using the base URL in the first response:

    ```
    $ curl -X GET -H "Accept: application/vnd.kafka.json.v2+json"
    http://localhost:8082/consumers/powerful_json_consumer/instances/powerful_consumer_instance/records
    [{"key":null,"value":{"employee":"1234"},"partition":0,"offset":0,"topic":"open_topic"}]
    ```

5. To close the consumer:

```
$ curl -X DELETE -H "Content-Type: application/vnd.kafka.v2+json" http://localhost:8082/consumers/powerful_json_consumer/instances/powerful_consumer_instance
```

There is no content in the response.

There's more...

Here are some administrative tasks, for example, to inspect metadata:

1. To get the list of topics:

```
$ curl "http://localhost:8082/topics"
["__consumer_offsets","_schemas","open_topic"]
```

2. To get info on one topic:

```
$ curl "http://localhost:8082/topics/open_topic"
{"name":"open_topic","configs":{},"partitions":[{"partition":0,"leader":0,"replicas":[{"broker":0,"leader":true,"in_sync":true}]}]}
```

3. To get info about a topic's partitions:

```
$ curl "http://localhost:8082/topics/open_topic/partitions"
[{"partition":0,"leader":0,"replicas":[{"broker":0,"leader":true,"in_sync":true}]}]
```

See also

- To see the full documentation of the Kafka REST Proxy, visit this URL: https://docs.confluent.io/current/kafka-rest/docs/intro.html

Using Kafka Connect

As mentioned, Kafka Connect is a framework used to connect Kafka with external systems such as key-value stores (think of Riak, Coherence, and Dynamo), databases (Cassandra), search indexes (Elastic), and filesystems (HDFS).

The Confluent Platform

In this book, there is a whole chapter about Kafka connectors, but this recipe is part of the Confluent Platform.

Getting ready

The Confluent Platform should be up and running:

```
$ confluent log connect
```

How to do it...

To read a data file with Kafka Connect:

1. To list the installed connectors:

   ```
   $ confluent list connectors
   Bundled Predefined Connectors (edit configuration under etc/):
     elasticsearch-sink
     file-source
     file-sink
     jdbc-source
     jdbc-sink
     hdfs-sink
     s3-sink
   ```

2. The configuration file is located at `./etc/kafka/connect-file-source.properties`. It has these values:
   - The instance name:

     ```
     name=file_source
     ```

   - The implementer class:

     ```
     connector.class=FileStreamSource
     ```

   - The number of tasks of this connector instance:

     ```
     tasks.max=1
     ```

- The input file:

    ```
    file=continuous.txt
    ```

- The name of the output topic:

    ```
    topic=connector-test
    ```

3. Edit `continuous.txt`; add the following content:

    ```
    This is the line 1
    This is the line 2
    This is the line 3
    This is the line 4
    ```

4. Load the file:

    ```
    $ confluent load file-source
    {
      "name": "file_source",
      "config": {
        "connector.class": "FileStreamSource",
        "tasks.max": "1",
        "file": "continuous.txt",
        "topics": "connector-test",
        "name": "file-source"
      },
      "tasks": []
    }
    ```

5. Check whether the connector is OK:

    ```
    $ confluent status connectors
    [
      "file-source"
    ]
    ```

6. Check the status of the task:

    ```
    $ confluent status file-source
    {
      "name": "file-source",
      "connector": {
        "state": "RUNNING",
        "worker_id": "10.110.30.20:8083"
      },
      "tasks": [
    ```

```
{
  "state": "RUNNING",
  "id": 0,
  "worker_id": "10.110.30.20:8083"
}
  ]
}
```

7. Finally, check the topic with a consumer to see the messages in the file:

```
$ kafka-console-consumer --bootstrap-server localhost:9092 --topic connector-test --from-beginning

This is the line 1
This is the line 2
This is the line 3
This is the line 4
```

There's more...

To write a data file with Kafka Connect, the configuration file is located at `./etc/kafka/connect-file-sink.properties`. It has the following values:

- The instance name:

    `name=file_sink`

- The implementer class:

    `connector.class=FileStreamSink`

- The number of tasks of this connector instance:

    `tasks.max=1`

- The output file:

    `file=the_sink.txt`

- The name of the output topic:

    `topic=connector-test`

Let's follow these steps:

1. Load the file:

    ```
    $ confluent load file-sink
    {
      "name": "file-sink",
      "config": {
        "connector.class": "FileStreamSink",
        "tasks.max": "1",
        "file": "the_sink.txt",
        "topics": "connector-test",
        "name": "file-sink"
      },
      "tasks": []
    }
    ```

2. Check whether the connector is OK:

    ```
    $ confluent status connectors
    [
      "file-source",
      "file-sink"
    ]
    ```

3. Check the status of the task:

    ```
    $ confluent status file-sink
    {
      "name": "file-sink",
      "connector": {
        "state": "RUNNING",
        "worker_id": "10.110.30.20:8083"
      },
      "tasks": [
        {
          "state": "RUNNING",
          "id": 0,
          "worker_id": "10.110.30.20:8083"
        }
      ]
    }
    ```

4. Finally, modify/add more content to the `continous.txt` file and see the result in `the_sink.txt`
5. To unload the connectors, run the following:

   ```
   $ confluent unload file-source
   $ confluent unload file-sink
   ```

6. To stop Kafka Connect and the worker:

   ```
   $ confluent stop connect
   The output is:
   Stopping connect
   connect is [DOWN]
   ```

See also

- To see the full documentation of Kafka Connect, visit this URL: https://docs.confluent.io/current/connect/index.html

6
Kafka Streams

This chapter covers the following recipes:

- Setting up the project
- Running the streaming application

Introduction

Life is not discrete; it is a continuous flow. The first four chapters were focused on how to deal with a data pipeline manipulating every message individually. But what happens when we need to find a pattern or make a calculation over a subset of messages?

In the data world, a stream is linked to the most important abstractions. A stream depicts a continuously updating and unbounded process. Here, *unbounded* means unlimited size. By definition, a stream is a fault-tolerant, replayable, and ordered sequence of immutable data records. A data record is defined as a key-value pair.

Before we proceed, some concepts need to be defined:

- **Stream processing application**: Any program that utilizes the Kafka streams library is known as a **stream processing application**.
- **Processor topology**: This is a topology that defines the computational logic of the data processing that a stream processing application requires to be performed. A topology is a graph of stream processors (nodes) connected by streams (edges).

    There are two ways to define a topology:

    - Via the low-level processor API
    - Via the Kafka streams DSL

- **Stream processor**: This is a node present in the processor topology. It represents a processing step in a topology and is used to transform data in streams. The standard operations—filter, join, map, and aggregations—are examples of stream processors available in Kafka streams.
- **Windowing**: Sometimes, data records are divided into time buckets by a stream processor to window the stream by time. This is usually required for aggregation and join operations.
- **Join**: When two or more streams are merged based on the keys of their data records, a new stream is generated. The operation that generates this new stream is called a **join**. A join over record streams is usually required to be performed on a windowing basis.
- **Aggregation**: A new stream is generated by combining multiple input records into a single output record, by taking one input stream. The operation that creates this new stream is known as **aggregation**. Examples of aggregations are sums and counts.

Setting up the project

This recipe sets the project to use Kafka streams in the Treu application project.

Getting ready

The project generated in the first four chapters is needed.

How to do it...

1. Open the `build.gradle` file on the Treu project generated in Chapter 4, *Message Enrichment*, and add these lines:

    ```
    apply plugin: 'java'
    apply plugin: 'application'

    sourceCompatibility = '1.8'

    mainClassName = 'treu.StreamingApp'

    repositories {
      mavenCentral()
    ```

```
    }
    version = '0.1.0'

    dependencies {
      compile 'org.apache.kafka:kafka-clients:1.0.0'
      compile 'org.apache.kafka:kafka-streams:1.0.0'
      compile 'org.apache.avro:avro:1.7.7'
    }

    jar {
      manifest {
        attributes 'Main-Class': mainClassName
      }

      from {
        configurations.compile.collect {
          it.isDirectory() ? it : zipTree(it)
        }
      } {
        exclude "META-INF/*.SF"
        exclude "META-INF/*.DSA"
        exclude "META-INF/*.RSA"
      }
    }
```

2. To rebuild the app, from the project root directory, run this command:

   $ gradle jar

   The output is something like:

   ```
   ...
   BUILD SUCCESSFUL
   Total time: 24.234 secs
   ```

3. As the next step, create a file called `StreamingApp.java` in the `src/main/java/treu` directory with the following contents:

   ```
   package treu;

   import org.apache.kafka.streams.StreamsBuilder;
   import org.apache.kafka.streams.Topology;

   import org.apache.kafka.streams.KafkaStreams;
   import org.apache.kafka.streams.StreamsConfig;
   ```

```
import org.apache.kafka.streams.kstream.KStream;

import java.util.Properties;

public class StreamingApp {

  public static void main(String[] args) throws Exception {

    Properties props = new Properties();
    props.put(StreamsConfig.APPLICATION_ID_CONFIG,
"streaming_app_id");// 1
    props.put(StreamsConfig.BOOTSTRAP_SERVERS_CONFIG,
"localhost:9092"); //2

    StreamsConfig config = new StreamsConfig(props); // 3
    StreamsBuilder builder = new StreamsBuilder(); //4

    Topology topology = builder.build();

    KafkaStreams streams = new KafkaStreams(topology, config);

    KStream<String, String> simpleFirstStream =
builder.stream("src-topic"); //5

    KStream<String, String> upperCasedStream =
simpleFirstStream.mapValues(String::toUpperCase); //6

    upperCasedStream.to("out-topic"); //7

    System.out.println("Streaming App Started");
    streams.start();
    Thread.sleep(30000);   //8
    System.out.println("Shutting down the Streaming App");
    streams.close();
  }
}
```

How it works...

Follow the comments in the code:

- In line //1, the APPLICATION_ID_CONFIG is an identifier for the app inside the broker
- In line //2, the BOOTSTRAP_SERVERS_CONFIG specifies the broker to use

- In line //3, the `StreamsConfig` object is created, it is built with the properties specified
- In line //4, the `StreamsBuilder` object is created, it is used to build a topology
- In line //5, when `KStream` is created, the input topic is specified
- In line //6, another `KStream` is created with the contents of the `src-topic` but in uppercase
- In line //7, the uppercase stream should write the output to `out-topic`
- In line //8, the application will run for 30 seconds

Running the streaming application

In the previous recipe, the first version of the streaming app was coded. Now, in this recipe, everything is compiled and executed.

Getting ready

The execution of the previous recipe of this chapter is needed.

How to do it...

The streaming app doesn't receive arguments from the command line:

1. To build the project, from the `treu` directory, run the following command:

    ```
    $ gradle jar
    ```

    If everything is OK, the output should be:

    ```
    ...
    BUILD SUCCESSFUL
    Total time: ...
    ```

2. To run the project, we have four different command-line windows. The following diagram shows what the arrangement of command-line windows should look like:

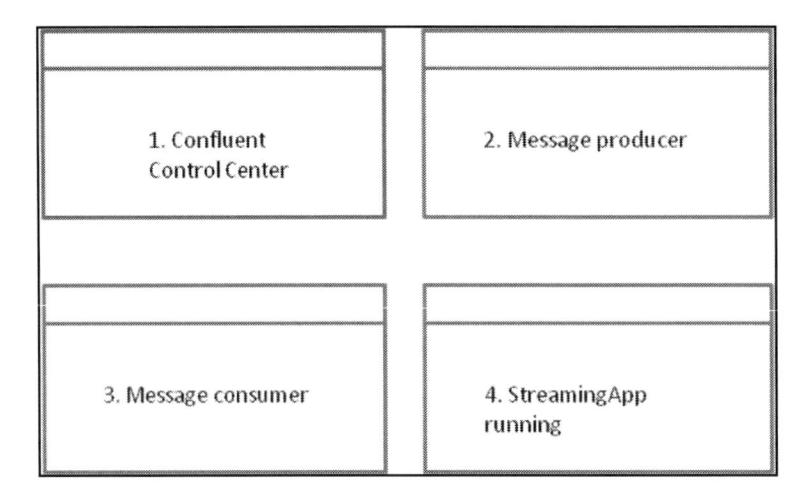

Figure 6.1: The four Terminals to test the streaming application—Confluent Control Center, Message producer, Message consumer, and the application itself

3. In the first command-line Terminal, run the control center:

   ```
   $ <confluent-path>/bin/confluent start
   ```

4. In the second command-line Terminal, create the two topics needed:

   ```
   $ bin/kafka-topics --create --topic src-topic --zookeeper localhost:2181 --partitions 1 --replication-factor 1
   $ bin/kafka-topics --create --topic out-topic --zookeeper localhost:2181 --partitions 1 --replication-factor 1
   ```

5. In that command-line Terminal, start the producer:

   ```
   $ bin/kafka-console-producer --broker-list localhost:9092 --topic src-topic
   ```

   This window is where the input messages are typed.

6. In the third command-line Terminal, start a consumer script listening to `out-topic`:

   ```
   $ bin/kafka-console-consumer --bootstrap-server localhost:9092 --from-beginning --topic out-topic
   ```

7. In the fourth command-line Terminal, start up the processing application. Go the project root directory (where the Gradle `jar` command was executed) and run:

   ```
   $ java -jar ./build/libs/treu-0.1.0.jar localhost:9092
   ```

8. Go to the second command-line Terminal (console-producer) and send the following three messages (remember to press *Enter* between messages and execute each one in just one line):

   ```
   $> Hello [Enter]
   $> Kafka [Enter]
   $> Streams [Enter]
   ```

9. The messages typed in console-producer should appear uppercase in the `out-topic` console consumer window:

   ```
   > HELLO
   > KAFKA
   > STREAMS
   ```

7
Managing Kafka

This chapter covers the following topics:

- Managing consumer groups
- Dumping log segments
- Importing ZooKeeper offsets
- Using the GetOffsetShell
- Using the JMX tool
- Using the MirrorMaker tool
- Replaying log producer
- Using state change log merger

Introduction

Managing an Apache Kafka cluster in production can be a difficult task. The Kafka authors have developed some command-line tools to make a DevOps team's life easier for debugging, testing, and running a Kafka cluster. This chapter covers some of these tools.

Managing consumer groups

The `ConsumerGroupCommand` tool is valuable when debugging consumer groups. This tool allows us to list, describe, and delete consumer groups.

Getting ready

For this recipe, Kafka must be installed, ZooKeeper running, the broker running, and some topics created on it. The topics should have produced some messages and have some consumers created in a consumer group. The point here is to get some information about the running consumers.

How to do it...

1. From the Kafka installation directory, run the following command:

   ```
   $ bin/kafka-consumer-groups.sh --bootstrap-server localhost:9092 --list
   ```

   The output is something like the following:

   ```
   Note: This will only show information about consumers that use the Java consumer API (non-ZooKeeper-based consumers).
       console-consumer-10354
       vipConsumersGroup
       console-consumer-44233
   ```

2. To see the offsets, use `describe` on the consumer group as follows:

   ```
   $ bin/kafka-consumer-groups.sh --bootstrap-server localhost:9092 --describe --group vipConsumersGroup
   Note: This will only show information about consumers that use the Java consumer API (non-ZooKeeper-based consumers).
       TOPIC           PARTITION   CURRENT-OFFSET   LOG-END-OFFSET   LAG
   CONSUMER-ID       HOST          CLIENT-ID
       source-topic    0           1                1                0
   consumer-1-be 4c31-e197-455b-89fb-cce53e380a26    /192.168.1.87
   consumer-1
   ```

3. As the command says, if old high-level consumers are used and the group metadata is stored in ZooKeeper (with the `offsets.storage =zookeeper` flag), specify `zookeeper` instead of `bootstrap-server`, as follows:

   ```
   $ bin/kafka-consumer-groups.sh --zookeeper localhost:2181 --list
   ```

How it works...

The `ConsumerGroupCommand` takes the following arguments:

- `--group <String: consumer group>`: This is the consumer group to manipulate
- `--bootstrap-server <String: server to connect>`: This is the server to connect to (for consumer groups based on a non-old consumer)
- `--zookeeper <String: urls>`: This is the ZooKeeper connection specified as a comma-separated list with elements in the form `host:port` (for consumer groups based on old consumers)
- `--topic <String: topic>`: This the topic that contains the consumer group information to manipulate
- `--list`: This lists all the consumer groups of the broker
- `--describe`: This describes the consumer group and lists the offset lag (number of messages not yet processed) on a given group
- `--reset-offsets`: This resets the offsets of the consumer group
- `--delete`: This is passed in a group to delete topic partition offsets and ownership information on the entire consumer group

Dumping log segments

This tool is for debugging the Kafka log data for various purposes, such as reviewing how the logs have been written and to see the status of the segments. Also, it is useful for reviewing the log files generated by Kafka.

Getting ready

For this recipe, Kafka must be installed, ZooKeeper running, broker running and some topics created on it. The topics should have produced some messages and have some consumers created in a consumer group. The point here is to have some information in the Kafka log segments, for debugging, auditing, or back up, as well as for checking log segment health.

How to do it...

1. From the Kafka installation directory, run the following command:

   ```
   $ bin/kafka-run-class.sh kafka.tools.DumpLogSegments --deep-
   iteration --files /tmp/kafka-logs/your-
   topic-0/00000000000000000000.log
   ```

   The output is something like the following:

   ```
   Dumping /tmp/kafka-logs/source-topic-0/00000000000000000000.log
   Starting offset: 0
   offset: 0 position: 0 CreateTime: 1511661360150 isvalid: true
   keysize: -1 valuesize: 4 magic: 2 compresscodec: NONE producerId:
   -1 sequence: -1 isTransactional: false headerKeys: []
   ```

How it works...

The `DumpLogSegments` command parses the log file and dumps its contents to the console; it is useful for debugging a seemingly corrupt log segment.

The `DumpLogSegments` command takes the following arguments:

- `--deep-iteration`: If set, it uses deep iteration (complete audit) instead of shallow iteration (superficial audit) to examine the log files.
- `--files <String: file1, file2, ...>`: This is a mandatory parameter. The comma-separated list of data log files to be dumped.
- `--max-message-size <Integer: size>`: This is used to offset the size of the largest message. The default value is `5242880`.
- `--print-data-log`: If it is set, the messages' content will be printed when dumping data logs.
- `--verify-index-only`: If it is set, this process just verifies the index log without printing its content.

Importing ZooKeeper offsets

Now we have a backup of the offsets contained in ZooKeeper at some point in time, one can restore them. This tool is handy for restoring the status of the offsets to the point when they were taken.

Getting ready

For this recipe, Kafka must be installed, ZooKeeper running, broker running, and some topics created on it. The topics should have produced some messages and have some consumers created. A file with the ZooKeeper offset previously exported is needed.

How to do it...

Let's assume that we have our offset status in the file, `/temp/zkoffset.txt`.

From the Kafka installation directory, run the following command:

```
$ bin/kafka-run-class.sh kafka.tools.ImportZkOffsets --inputfile
/tmp/zkoffset.txt --zkconnect localhost:2181
```

How it works...

The preceding command takes the following arguments:

- `--zkconnect`: This specifies the ZooKeeper connect string. It is a comma-separated list in the `host:port` format.
- `--input-file`: This specifies the file to import ZooKeeper offsets from.
- `--help`: This prints the help message.

Using the GetOffsetShell

When debugging an Apache Kafka project, it is sometimes useful to obtain the offset values of the topics. For this purpose, this tool comes in handy.

Getting ready

For this recipe, Kafka must be installed, ZooKeeper running, broker running, and some topics created on it. The topics should have produced some messages and have some consumers created.

How to do it...

From the Kafka installation directory, run the following command:

```
$ bin/kafka-run-class.sh kafka.tools.GetOffsetShell --broker-list
localhost:9092 --topic source-topic --time -1
```

The output is something like the following:

```
source-topic:0:0
source-topic:1:0
source-topic:2:6
source-topic:3:0
```

How it works...

The `GetOffsetShell` is an interactive shell to get the consumer offsets and takes the following options:

- `--broker-list <String: hostname:port>`: This specifies the list of server ports to connect to in a comma-separated list in the `host:port` format.
- `--max-wait-ms <Integer: ms>`: This specifies the maximum amount of time each fetch request has to wait. The default value is `1000`, that is 1 second.
- `--offsets <Integer: count>`: This specifies the number of offsets returned. By default `1`, only one offset.
- `--partitions <String: partition ids>`: It is a comma-separated list of partition IDs. If it is not specified, it fetches the offsets for all the partitions.
- `--time <Long: timestamp>`: It specifies the timestamp of the offsets fetched. `-1` for the latest and `-2` for the earliest.
- `--topic <String: topic>`: This is mandatory and it specifies the topic to fetch the offset.

Using the JMX tool

JMX is Java management extensions. For the seasoned Java user, JMX is a technology that provides the tools for managing and monitoring the JVM. Kafka has its own JMX tool to get the JMX reports in an easy way.

Getting ready

For this recipe, Kafka must be installed, ZooKeeper running, broker running, and some topics created on it. The topics should have produced some messages and have some consumers created.

How to do it...

From the Kafka installation directory, run the following command:

```
$ bin/kafka-run-class.sh kafka.tools.JmxTool --jmx-url
service:jmx:rmi:///jndi/rmi://:9999/jmxrmi
```

How it works...

The JMX tool dumps the JMX values to standard output. The JMX tool takes the following parameters:

- `--attributes <String: name>`: This is a comma-separated list of objects with a whitelist of attributes to be queried. All the objects are reported if none are mentioned.
- `--date-format <String: format>`: This specifies the data format to be used for the `time` field. The available options are the same as those for `java.text.SimpleDateFormat`.
- `--help`: This prints the help message.
- `--jmx-url <String: service-url>`: This specifies the URL to connect to the poll JMX data. The default value is:
  `service:jmx:rmi:///jndi/rmi://:9999/jmxrmi`.
- `--object-name <String: name>`: This specifies the JMX object name to be used as a query, it can contain wild cards. If no objects are specified, all the objects will be queried.
- `--reporting-interval <Integer: ms>`: This specifies the interval in milliseconds with the poll JMX stats. The default value is `2000`, that is 2 seconds.

Managing Kafka

There's more...

JMX is a vast topic and beyond the scope of this book. To view JMX data, there is a popular tool called JConsole. To use JConsole, just type the command `$ jconsole` in a machine with Java installed.

For more information, visit the JConsole page: https://docs.oracle.com/javase/8/docs/technotes/guides/management/jconsole.html.

Using the MirrorMaker tool

The MirrorMaker tool is useful when we need to replicate the same data in a different cluster. The MirrorMaker tool continuously copies data between two Kafka clusters.

Getting ready

For this recipe, we need two different instances of Kafka running in different clusters. The objective is to replicate the data from one to the other.

How to do it...

From the Kafka installation directory, run this command:

```
$ bin/kafka-run-class.sh kafka.tools.MirrorMaker --consumer.config
config/consumer.config --producer.config config/producer.config --whitelist
source-topic
```

How it works...

The MirrorMaker tool takes the following parameters:

- `--blacklist <String: Java regex(String)>`: This specifies the blacklist of topics to be mirrored. This can be a regular expression as well.
- `--consumer.config <String: config file>`: This specifies the path to the consumer configuration file to consume from a source cluster. Multiple files may be specified.

- `--help`: This prints the help message.
- `--new.consumer`: This is used to create a new consumer in MirrorMaker (it is set by default).
- `--num.streams <Integer: Number of threads>`: This indicates the number of consumption streams (default: 1).
- `--producer.config <String: config file>`: This specifies the path to the embedded producer configuration file.
- `--whitelist <String: Java regex(String)>`: This specifies the whitelist of topics to be mirrored.

There's more...

To understand how Kafka mirroring works,
visit: https://cwiki.apache.org/confluence/pages/viewpage.action?pageId=27846330.

See also

- This page contains a comparison between MirrorMaker and the confluent replicator: https://docs.confluent.io/current/multi-dc/mirrormaker.html

Replaying log producer

The `ReplayLogProducer` tool is used to move data from one topic to another.

Getting ready

For this recipe, Kafka must be installed, ZooKeeper running, broker running, and some topics created on it. The topics should have produced some messages. The source topic and the destination topic are required.

How to do it...

From the Kafka installation directory, run this command:

```
$ bin/kafka-run-class.sh kafka.tools.ReplayLogProducer --sync --broker-list
localhost:9092 --inputtopic source-topic --outputtopic good-topic --
zookeeper localhost:2181
```

How it works...

The `ReplayLogProducer` takes the following parameters:

- `--broker-list <String: hostname:port>`: This is a mandatory parameter. It specifies the broker list.
- `--inputtopic <String: input-topic>`: This is a mandatory parameter. It specifies the source topic.
- `--messages <Integer: count>`: This specifies the number of messages to send. The default value is -1, meaning infinite.
- `--outputtopic <String: output-topic>`: This is a mandatory parameter. It specifies the destination topic.
- `--reporting-interval <Integer: ms>`: This specifies the interval in milliseconds to print the progress information. The default value is five seconds.
- `--threads <Integer: threads>`: This specifies the number of working threads. By default, just one thread is used.
- `--sync`: If it is specified, the messages are sent synchronously, if not they are sent asynchronously.
- `--zookeeper <String: zookeeper url>`: This is a mandatory parameter. It specifies the connection string for the ZooKeeper connection in the `host:port` format. Specify multiple URLs to allow a fail-over mechanism.

Using state change log merger

The `StateChangeLogMerger` tool merges the state change logs from different brokers for easy posterior analysis. It is a tool for merging the log files from several brokers to rebuild a unified history of what happened.

Getting ready

For this recipe, Kafka must be installed, ZooKeeper running, brokers running, and some topics created on it. The topics should have produced some messages. It is better if there are several days' worth of broker information.

How to do it...

From the Kafka installation directory, run this command:

```
$ bin/kafka-run-class.sh kafka.tools.StateChangeLogMerger --log-regex
/tmp/state-change.log* --partitions 0,1,2 --topic source-topic
```

How it works...

The `StateChangeLogMerger` command takes the following parameters:

- `--end-time <String: end>`: This specifies the latest timestamp of state change entries to be merged in `java.text.SimpleDateFormat`
- `--logs <String: file1, file2, ...>`: This is used to specify a comma-separated list of state change logs or regex for the log filenames
- `--logs-regex <String: regex>`: This is used to specify a regex to match the state change log files to be merged
- `--partitions <String: 0, 1, 2, ...>`: This specifies a comma-separated list of partition IDs whose state change logs should be merged
- `--start-time <String: start>`: This specifies the earliest timestamp of state change entries to be merged in `java.text.SimpleDateFormat`
- `--topic <String: topic>`: This specifies the topic whose state change logs should be merged

This chapter has covered some system tools to manage Apache Kafka. The source code for these tools can be found at: https://github.com/apache/kafka/tree/1.0/core/src/main/scala/kafka/tools.

A brief description of these tools can be found at: https://cwiki.apache.org/confluence/display/KAFKA/System+Tools.

8
Operating Kafka

This chapter covers the following topics:

- Adding or removing topics
- Modifying message topics
- Implementing a graceful shutdown
- Balancing leadership
- Expanding clusters
- Increasing the replication factor
- Decommissioning brokers
- Checking the consumer position

Introduction

This chapter explains the different operations that can be done on a Kafka cluster. These tools cannot be used daily, but they help the DevOps team manage the Kafka clusters.

Adding or removing topics

The first chapters explained how to create a topic. The power behind the tool is that it can add topics programmatically or manually, and can enable the Kafka option to automatically add topics. In production, it is recommended that you disable automatic topic creation to eliminate programming errors where data is accidentally pushed to a topic that it didn't mean to create at the beginning.

Getting ready

For this recipe, Kafka must be installed, ZooKeeper should be running, and the broker should be running with some topics created on it.

How to do it...

1. Go to the Kafka installation directory and create a topic called `test-topic`:

   ```
   $ bin/kafka-topics.sh --create --zookeeper localhost:2181 --topic test-topic --partitions 5 --replication-factor 2
   ```

   The output should be as follows:

   ```
   Created topic "test-topic".
   ```

2. Describe the `test-topic` topic with the following command:

   ```
   $ bin/kafka-topics.sh --describe --zookeeper localhost:2181 --topic test-topic
   ```

   The output should be as follows:

   ```
   topic:test-topic   PartitionCount:10 ReplicationFactor:2
   Configs:
           Topic: test-topic Partition: 0     Leader: 0   Replicas: 0 Isr: 0
           Topic: test-topic Partition: 1     Leader: 0   Replicas: 0 Isr: 0
           Topic: test-topic Partition: 2     Leader: 0   Replicas: 0 Isr: 0
           Topic: test-topic Partition: 3     Leader: 0   Replicas: 0 Isr: 0
           Topic: test-topic Partition: 4     Leader: 0   Replicas: 0 Isr: 0
   ```

3. Delete the `test-topic` with the following command:

   ```
   $ bin/kafka-topics.sh --delete --zookeeper localhost:2181 --topic test-topic
   ```

The output should be as follows:

```
Topic test-topic is marked for deletion.
Note: This command will not have impact if delete.topic.enable in
configuration file is not set to true.
```

How it works...

The replication factor indicates how many servers replicate each message that is written. For example, if the replication factor is four, it indicates that three servers can fail before the data is lost. It is recommended to use a replication factor greater than one to reboot the machines without interrupting the service.

The partition number indicates how many logs the topic will be divided into. Remember that each partition must fit entirely on a single server. It is clear that if four partitions are specified, the topic will be handled by no more than four servers. The partition number also impacts the parallelism of the consumers.

Each partition has its own directory under the Kafka log directory. This directory name (log.dir and log.dirs are specified in the config/server.properties) consists of the topic name followed by a dash and the partition ID. The directory name cannot be over 255 characters long, limiting the topic name length.

The kafka-topics shell takes parameters; some are explained as follows:

- --create: This is specified to create a topic.
- --delete: This is specified to delete a topic. The server configuration must have delete.topic.enable=true. By default, this is set as true. When it is false, the topic cannot be deleted.
- --describe: This lists the details for the given topics.
- --if-exists: This parameter is used when altering or deleting topics; the action will only execute if the topic exists.
- --if-not-exists: This parameter is used when creating topics; the action will only execute if the topic does not already exist.
- --list: This is specified to list all topics.
- --topic <String: name>: This specifies the topic name.
- --partitions <Integer: num>: This is used to specify the number of partitions to be created for the topic.

- `--replication-factor <Integer: num>`: This specifies the number of replicas to be created for the topic. As explained, this number must be less than the number of nodes in the cluster.
- `--zookeeper <String: urls>`: This specifies the ZooKeeper connect string; it is a comma-separated list in the format, `host:port`.

Other configurations needed for the topic can be specified by using the following conventions:

- `--config <String: name=value>`: This is used to override the default properties set on the server
- `--delete-config <String: name>`: This specifies that a topic configuration override be removed for an existing topic

There's more...

Many more configuration options are available. These have been detailed at `http://kafka.apache.org/documentation/#configuration`.

See also

- Check broker configuration in Chapter 1, *Configuring Kafka*, for how to set topic defaults at the broker level

Modifying message topics

Once created, topics can be modified. For example, when a new node is added to the cluster or a different parallelism is needed. Sometimes, deleting the topic and starting over is not the correct solution.

Getting ready

For this recipe, Kafka must be installed, ZooKeeper should be running, and the broker should be running with some topics created on it.

How to do it...

1. Run the following command from the Kafka installation directory:

   ```
   $ bin/kafka-topics.sh --zookeeper localhost:2181/chroot --alter --topic test-topic --partitions 40 --config delete.retention.ms=10000 --delete-config retention.ms
   ```

   This command changes the `delete.retention.ms` to 10 seconds and deletes the configuration `retention.ms`

   > **TIP**: Kafka does not support reducing the number of partitions for a topic.

There is the `kafka-configs` shell; the syntax to add and remove is as follows:

2. To add a config to a topic, run the following:

   ```
   $ bin/kafka-configs.sh --zookeeper host:port/chroot --entity-type topics --entity-name topic_name --alter --add-config x=y
   ```

3. To remove a config from a topic, run the following:

   ```
   $ bin/kafka-configs.sh --zookeeper host:port/chroot --entity-type topics --entity-name topic_name --alter --delete-config x
   ```

How it works...

So, there are two shells to change a topic configuration. The first is `kafka-topics` (explained in a previous recipe), and the second is `kafka-configs`.

The `kafka-configs` shell takes parameters; some are explained here:

- `--add-config<String>`: This is the configuration to add, in a comma-separated list in the format `k1=v1,k2=[v1,v2,v2],k3=v3`.
- `--alter`: This is used to modify a configuration for an entity.
- `--delete-config <String>`: This is the configuration to be removed (comma-separated list).

Operating Kafka

- `--describe`: This parameter lists the current configurations for the given entity.
- `--entity-name <String>`: This is the name of the entity.
- `--entity-type <String>`: This is the type of the entity; it could be topics, clients, users, or brokers.
- `--zookeeper <String: urls>`: This is a mandatory parameter and specifies the ZooKeeper connect string. It is a comma-separated list in the format `host:port`.

There's more...

Recall that `kafka-configs.sh` is not just for topics; it can also be used to modify the configuration of clients, users, and brokers.

See also

- More configuration options are available. These have been detailed at http://kafka.apache.org/documentation/#topicconfigs.

Implementing a graceful shutdown

In production, you may experience an abrupt shutdown caused by inevitable circumstances; for example, a power outage or a sudden machine reboot. But more often, there are planned shutdowns for machine maintenance or configuration changes. In these situations, the smooth shutdown of a node in the cluster is desirable, maintaining the cluster up and running without data loss.

Getting ready

For this recipe, Kafka must be installed.

How to do it...

1. First, edit the Kafka configuration file in `config/server.properties` and add the following line:

   ```
   controlled.shutdown.enable=true
   ```

2. Start all the nodes
3. With all the cluster nodes running, shut down one broker with the following command in the Kafka installation directory:

   ```
   $ bin/kafka-server-stop.sh
   ```

How it works...

If the setting for a controlled shutdown is enabled, it ensures that a server shutdown happens properly as follows:

- It writes all the logs to disk so that there are no issues with logs when you restart the broker
- If this node is the leader, it makes sure that another node becomes the leader for a partition

This ensures that each partition's downtime is reduced considerably.

It is important to say that a controlled shutdown will only succeed if all the partitions hosted on the broker have replicas (a replication factor greater than one and at least one replica alive).

Balancing leadership

A leader broker of a topic partition can be crashed or stopped, and then the leadership is transferred to another replica. This might produce an imbalance in the lead Kafka brokers (an imbalance is when the leader is dead or unreachable). To recover from this imbalance, we need **balancing leadership**.

Getting ready

For this recipe, a Kafka cluster setup with several nodes is needed. One of the Kafka nodes is down, and subsequently, it is restored.

How to do it...

Run the following command from the Kafka installation directory:

```
$ bin/kafka-preferred-replica-election.sh --zookeeperlocalhost:2181/chroot
```

How it works...

If the list of replicas for a partition is [3, 5, 8], then node 3 is preferred as the leader, rather than nodes 5 or 8. This is because it is earlier in the replica list. By running this command, we tell the Kafka cluster to try to restore leadership to the restored replicas.

To explain how it works, suppose that after the leader stops, new Kafka nodes join the cluster. This command avoids running them as slaves without direct operations assigned and redistributes the load among the available nodes.

The command takes the following parameter:

- `--zookeeper <String: urls>`: This is the mandatory parameter. It specifies the ZooKeeper connect string and is a comma-separated list in the format `host:port`. This parameter is useful if you have more than one Kafka cluster using the same ZooKeeper cluster.

There's more...

So we don't have to execute this command continuously, configure Kafka to do this automatically by turning this flag on in the configuration:

```
auto.leader.rebalance.enable = true
```

Expanding clusters

Adding nodes to an existing cluster is not the same as building a new Kafka cluster. Adding nodes to an existing cluster is easy. We do this by assigning them a unique broker ID, but they are not going to receive data automatically. A cluster reconfiguration is needed to indicate which partition replicas go where. Then, the partitions will move to the newly added nodes. This recipe shows how to do that.

Getting ready

For this recipe, Kafka must be installed, ZooKeeper should be running, and the broker should be running with some topics created on it.

How to do it...

1. This recipe moves all partitions for existing topics: `topic_1` and `topic_2`. The newly generated brokers are `broker_7` and `broker_8` (suppose that brokers 1 to 6 already exist). After finishing the movement, all partitions for `topic_1` and `topic_2` will exist only in `broker_7` and `broker_8`.

2. The tool only accepts JSON files as input; let's create the JSON file as follows:

    ```
    $ cat to_reassign.json

    {"topics": [{"topic": "topic_1"},
                {"topic": "topic_2"}],
    "version":1
    }
    ```

3. When the JSON file is ready, use the partition reassignment tool to generate the assignment (note it will not be executed yet) with the following command:

    ```
    $ bin/kafka-reassign-partitions.sh --zookeeper localhost:2181 --topics-to-move-json-file to_reassign.json --broker-list "7,8" --generate
    ```

The output is something like this:

```
Current partition replica assignment
{"version":1,
"partitions":[{"topic":"topic_1","partition":0,"replicas":[1,2]},

{"topic":"topic_1","partition":1,"replicas":[3,4]},

{"topic":"topic_1","partition":2,"replicas":[5,6]},

{"topic":"topic_2","partition":0,"replicas":[1,2]},

{"topic":"topic_2","partition":1,"replicas":[3,4]},

{"topic":"topic_2","partition":2,"replicas":[5,6]}]
}
Proposed partition reassignment configuration
{"version":1,
"partitions":[{"topic":"topic_1","partition":0,"replicas":[7,8]},

{"topic":"topic_1","partition":1,"replicas":[7,8]},

{"topic":"topic_1","partition":2,"replicas":[7,8]},

{"topic":"topic_2","partition":0,"replicas":[7,8]},

{"topic":"topic_2","partition":1,"replicas":[7,8]},

{"topic":"topic_2","partition":2,"replicas":[7,8]}]
}
```

Remember that it is just a proposal; no changes have been made to the cluster yet. The final reassignment should be specified in a new JSON file.

4. Once we have generated a new configuration, make some changes from the proposal. Create a new JSON file with the output of the previous step. Modify the destinations of the different partitions.
5. Write a JSON file (custom-assignment.json) to move each particular partition to each specific node as needed:

```
{"version":1,
"partitions":[ {"topic":"topic_1","partition":0,"replicas":[7,8]},

{"topic":"topic_1","partition":1,"replicas":[7,8]},

{"topic":"topic_1","partition":2,"replicas":[7,8]},
```

```
{"topic":"topic_2","partition":0,"replicas":[7,8]},

{"topic":"topic_2","partition":1,"replicas":[7,8]}]

{"topic":"topic_2","partition":2,"replicas":[7,8]},
     }
```

6. Now, to execute the reassignment, run the following command from the Kafka installation directory:

```
$ bin/kafka-reassign-partitions.sh --zookeeper localhost:2181 --reassignment-json-file custom-assignment.json --execute
```

The output is something like this:

```
    Save this to use as the --reassignment-json-file option during rollback
    Successfully started reassignment of partitions
    {"version":1,
"partitions":[{"topic":"topic_1","partition":0,"replicas":[7,8]},

{"topic":"topic_1","partition":1,"replicas":[7,8]},

{"topic":"topic_1","partition":2,"replicas":[7,8]},

{"topic":"topic_2","partition":0,"replicas":[7,8]},

{"topic":"topic_2","partition":1,"replicas":[7,8]}]

{"topic":"topic_2","partition":2,"replicas":[7,8]},
     }
```

7. Now, run the same command to verify the partition assignment:

```
$ bin/kafka-reassign-partitions.sh --zookeeper localhost:2181 --reassignment-json-file custom-assignment.json --verify
```

The output is something like this:

```
Status of partition reassignment:
Reassignment of partition [topic_1,0] completed successfully
Reassignment of partition [topic_1,1] completed successfully
Reassignment of partition [topic_1,2] is in progress
Reassignment of partition [topic_2,0] completed successfully
Reassignment of partition [topic_2,1] is in progress
Reassignment of partition [topic_2,2] is in progress
```

How it works...

The first step creates a JSON file with the topics to reassign.

The second step generates a candidate configuration for the specified Kafka topics using the reassign partitions tool. This tool takes the following parameters:

- `--broker-list <String: brokerlist>`: These are the brokers to which the partitions need to be reassigned, in the form 0, 1, 2. Required if `--topics-to-move-json-file` is used to generate reassignment configuration.
- `--execute`: This is used to start the reassignment, as specified in `--reassignment-json-file`.
- `--generate`: This is used to generate a candidate partition reassignment configuration. As seen, it does not execute it.
- `--reassignment-json-file <String: file>`: This is the JSON filename of the partition reassignment configuration.
- `--topics-to-move-json-file <String: file>`: This is used to generate a new assignment configuration, moving the partitions of the specified topics to the list of brokers indicated by the `--broker-list` option.
- `--verify`: This is used to verify whether the new assignment has completed as specified in the `--reassignment-json-file`.
- `--zookeeper <String: urls>`: This is a mandatory parameter: the connection string for the ZooKeeper connection, in the form `host:port`. Multiple URLs mean allowing fail-over.

The execute step will start moving data from the original replica to the new ones. It will take time, based on how much data is being moved. Finally, to check the status of the movement, run the verify command. It will display the current status of the different partitions.

There's more...

To perform a rollback, just save the configuration generated in step 2 and apply this recipe, moving the topics to the original configuration.

Increasing the replication factor

In cases where more machines are added to the Kafka cluster, increasing the replication factor means moving replicas for a topic to these new machines.

Getting ready

For this recipe, Kafka must be installed, ZooKeeper running, and the broker running with some topics created on it with some replicas. Start new nodes and add them to this cluster.

How to do it...

This example increases the replication factor of partition 0 of the topic `topic_1` from 2 to 4. Before the increment, the partition's only replica existed on brokers 3 and 4. This example adds more replicas on brokers 5 and 6.

1. Create a JSON file named `increase-replication.json` with this code:

   ```
   $cat increase-replication.json
   {"version":1,
   "partitions":[{"topic":"topic_1","partition":0,"replicas":[3,4,5,6]
   }]}
   ```

2. Then, run the following command:

   ```
   $ bin/kafka-reassign-partitions.sh --zookeeper localhost:2181 --reassignment-json-file increase-replication-factor.json --execute
   ```

How it works...

At the beginning, `topic_1` was created, with replication factor 2. The cluster has the brokers 3 and 4. Now, we have added more brokers to the cluster, called 5 and 6.

The JSON file we created indicates the partitions to be modified. In the JSON file, we indicated the topic, partition ID, and the list of replica brokers. Once it executes, the new Kafka brokers will start replicating the topic.

The parameters this command takes are indicated in the previous recipe.

Operating Kafka

There's more...

To verify the status of the reassignment, run the following command:

```
$ bin/kafka-reassign-partitions.sh --zookeeper localhost:2181 --reassignment-json-file increase-replication.json --verify
```

Decommissioning brokers

As Kafka clusters can be expanded, they can also be shortened. There are cases where it is necessary to remove some nodes. Removing some Kafka nodes from a cluster is called **decommissioning**. Decommissioning is not automatic; some reassignment must be applied to allow replicas to move to the live brokers.

Getting ready

For this recipe, Kafka must be installed, ZooKeeper running, and a Kafka cluster running with at least three nodes. A topic called `topic_1` with replication factor 3 should be running on the cluster.

How to do it...

1. First, gracefully shut down the broker to be removed
2. Once it is shut down, create a JSON file named `change-replication.json` with the following content:

   ```
   {"version":1,
   "partitions":[{"topic":"topic_1","partition":0,"replicas":[1,2]}]}
   ```

3. Reassign the topic to the two living brokers with the `reassign-partitions` command:

   ```
   $ bin/kafka-reassign-partitions.sh --zookeeper localhost:2181 --reassignment-json-file change-replication.json --execute
   ```

How it works...

After shutting down the node, proceed with the decommission of the partitions of that broker.

Internally, the shutdown steps are as follows:

1. The logs for all the lead partitions on that node are flushed to disk
2. After the lead is transferred, the node is finally shut down

In the JSON file, we specify which partition must be part of which replica. Obviously, we are removing all references to the decommissioned node.

Running the command will update the partition replication information in the Kafka cluster with the instructions in the JSON file.

Checking the consumer position

Sometimes, it is useful to check the customer's offset position. Here is a tool to check how much the consumers are lagging from the produced messages.

Getting ready

For this recipe, Kafka must be installed, ZooKeeper running, and the broker running with some topics created on it. Also, a consumer must be running to read from this topic.

How to do it...

Run the following command from the Kafka directory:

```
$ bin/kafka-consumer-groups.sh --bootstrap-server localhost:9092 --describe --group vipConsumersGroup
```

The output is something like the following:

```
     TOPIC   PARTITION   CURRENT-OFFSET   LOG-END-OFFSET   LAG   CONSUMER-ID
HOST                                      CLIENT-ID
    source-topic                    0                1       1
0           consumer-1-beff4c31-e197-455b-89fb-cce53e380a26    /192.168.1.87
consumer-1
```

How it works...

The `Kafka-Consumer-Groups` command takes the following arguments:

- `--group <String: consumer group>`: This is the consumer group to manipulate
- `--bootstrap-server <String: server to connect>`: This is the server to connect to (for consumer groups based on non-old consumers)
- `--zookeeper <String: urls>`: This is the ZooKeeper connection, specified as a comma-separated list with elements in the form `host:port` (for consumer groups based on old consumers)
- `--topic <String: topic>`: This is the topic whose consumer group information we manipulate
- `--list` : This lists all the consumer groups of the broker
- `--describe`: This describes the consumer group and lists the offset lag (number of messages not yet processed) on a given group
- `--reset-offsets`: This resets the offsets of the consumer group
- `--delete`: This is passed into a group to delete topic partition offsets and ownership information on the entire consumer group

This chapter has covered some system tools to operate Apache Kafka. The following chapter is about how to implement monitoring and security in Kafka.

9
Monitoring and Security

This chapter covers the following topics:

- Monitoring server statistics
- Monitoring producer statistics
- Monitoring consumer statistics
- Monitoring with the help of Graphite
- Monitoring with the help of Ganglia
- Implementing authentication using SSL
- Implementing authentication using SASL/Kerberos

Introduction

This chapter covers two important themes: monitoring and security. Knowing whether a Kafka cluster is working correctly in production is critical. Sometimes, just knowing that the cluster is up is enough, but checking throughput and latencies is also important. Kafka exposes important statistics for monitoring purposes. The first part of the chapter talks about various statistics and how they are exposed, as well as how to monitor them with tools such as Graphite and Ganglia.

The second part of the chapter is about security: in a nutshell, how to implement SSL authentication, SASL/Kerberos authentication, and SASL/plain authentication.

Monitoring server statistics

Kafka exposes monitoring statistics using Yammer metrics. Yammer metrics is a protocol that exposes six types of metrics: gauges, counters, meters, histograms, timers, and health checks. This recipe shows how to monitor the metrics exposed by Kafka from the server side. In the following recipes, we cover the producer and consumer related metrics.

Getting ready

For this recipe, we just need a Kafka broker up and running.

To set the JMX port, from the Kafka installation directory start the broker using the following command:

```
$ JMX_PORT=10101 bin/kafka-server-start.sh config/server.properties
```

Also, JConsole must be installed, check the installation with the following command:

```
$ jconsole
```

How to do it...

1. Run JConsole using the following command:

   ```
   $ jconsole 127.0.0.1:10101
   ```

Chapter 9

2. In the following screenshot, we can see all the different parameters plotted over time:

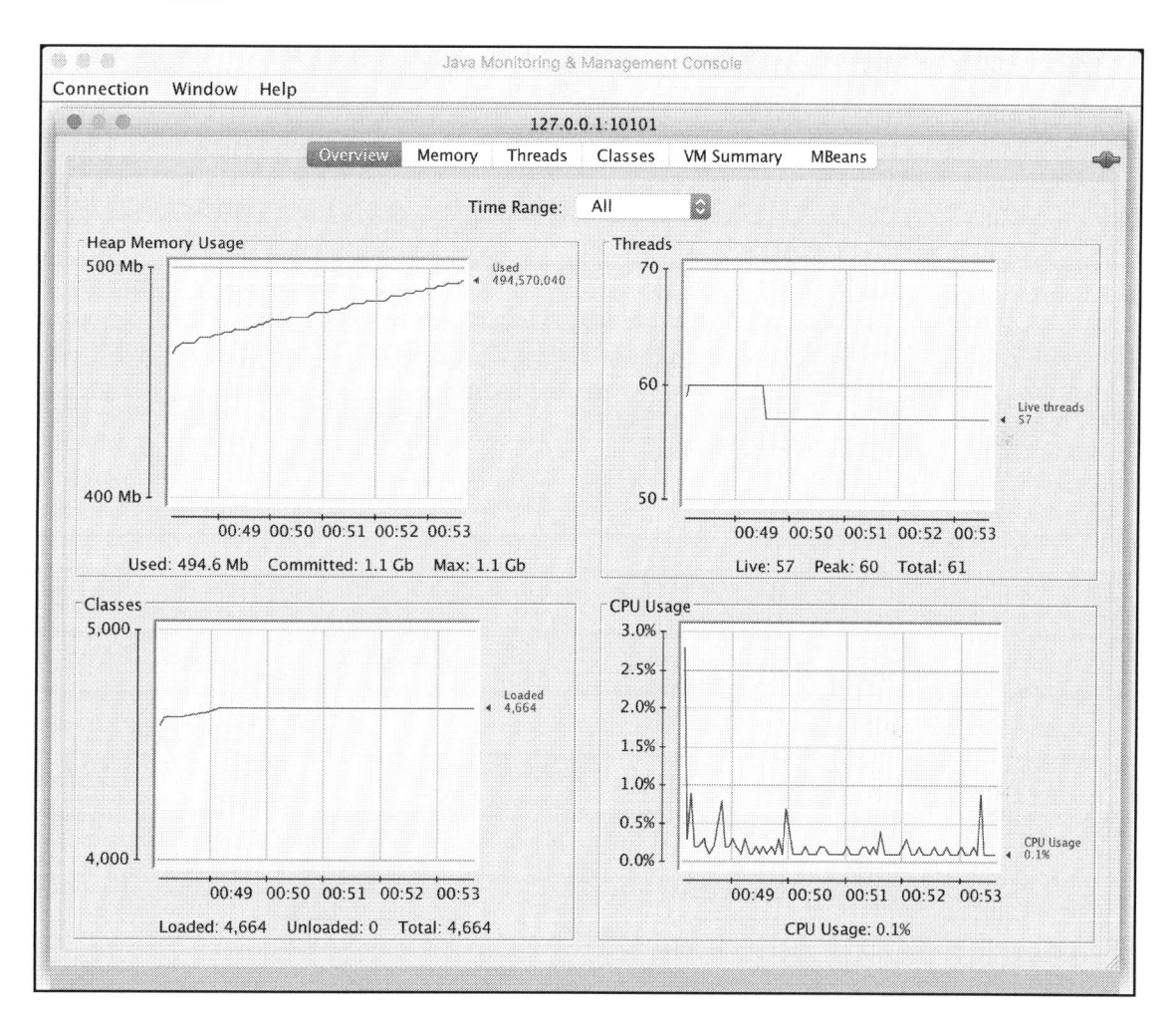

Figure 9.1: JConsole after executing command: jconsole 127.0.0.1:10101

Monitoring and Security

3. Switch to the **MBeans** tab and expand the Kafka server metrics:

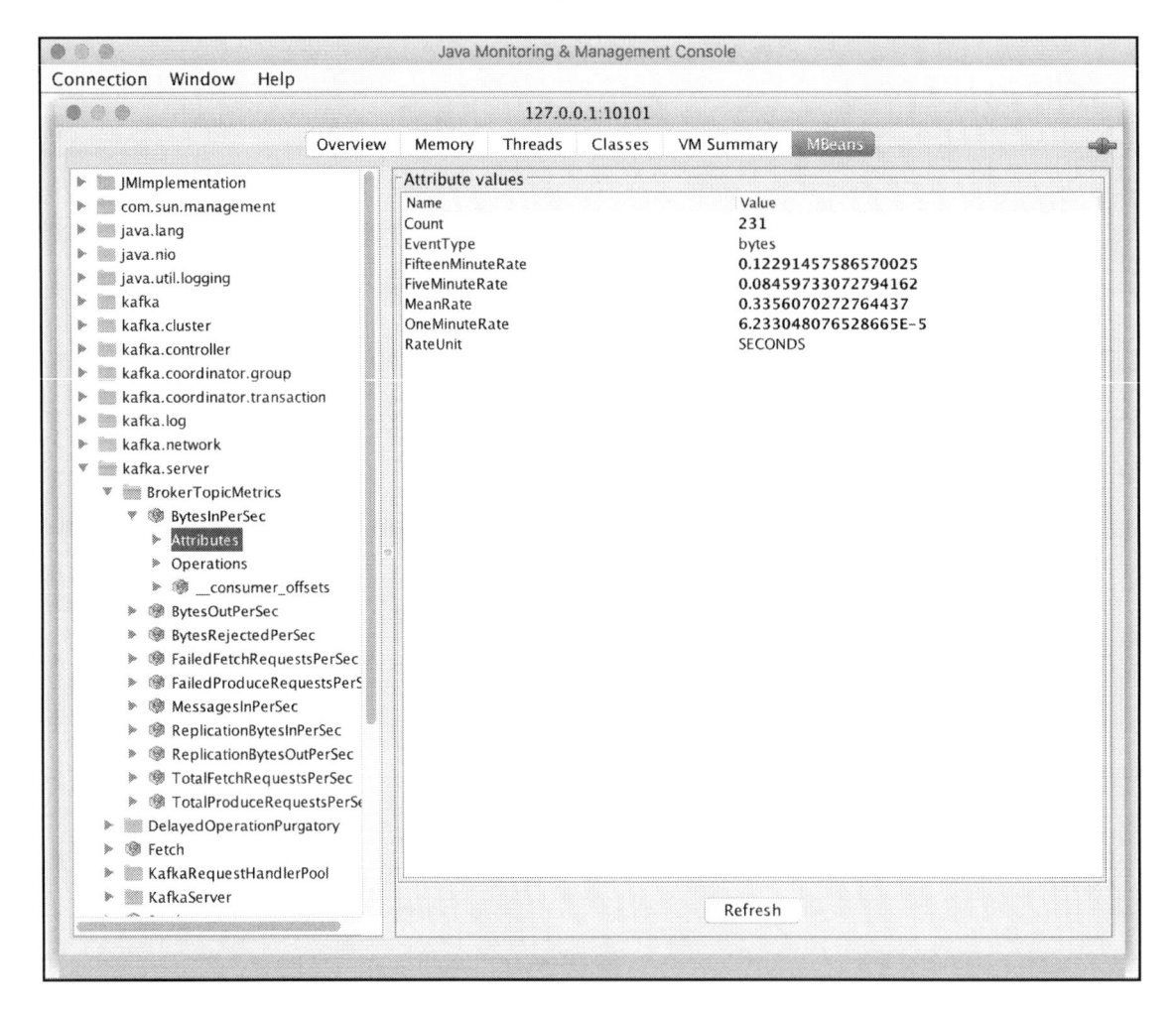

Figure 9.2: JConsole MBeans tab with the Kafka server metrics

The values of all the Kafka metrics are available for analysis.

How it works...

The JConsole application connects to the JMX port exposed by Kafka. Using JConsole, all the metrics can be read. The details of the metrics exposed by Kafka with the MBean object name are as follows:

- `kafka.server:type=BrokerTopicMetrics,name=MessagesInPerSec`: This gives the number of messages inserted in Kafka per second. It has the attribute values given as counts: minute rate, 5 minute rate, 15 minute rate, and mean rate.
- `kafka.server:type=ReplicaManager,name=UnderReplicatedPartition`: This specifies the number of partitions for the number of replica criteria not met. If this value is greater than zero, it means the cluster has issues replicating the partitions as planned.
- `kafka.controller:type=KafkaController,name=ActiveControllerCount`: This gives the number of active Kafka controllers for reelection.
- `kafka.controller:type=ControllerStats,name=LeaderElectionRateAndTimeMs`: This gives values of the rate at which leader election takes place and the latencies involved in that process. It gives latencies as percentiles: 50, 75, 95, 98, 99, and 99.9. It also gives the time taken for leader election as: minute rate, 5 minute rate, and 15 minute rate. It also gives the count.
- `kafka.controller:type=ControllerStats,name=UncleanLeaderElectionsPerSec`: This gives statistics of unclean leader election. It can give these values as a mean, 1 minute rate, 5 minute rate, and 15 minute rate. It also gives the count.
- `kafka.server:type=ReplicaManager,name=PartitionCount`: This gives the total number of partitions in that particular Kafka node.
- `kafka.server:type=ReplicaManager,name=LeaderCount`: This gives the total number of leader partitions in that particular Kafka node.
- `kafka.server:type=ReplicaManager,name=IsrShrinksPerSec`: This specifies the rate at which in-sync replicas shrink. It can give these values as a mean, minute rate, 5 minute rate, and 15 minute rate. It also gives the count of events.
- `kafka.server:type=ReplicaManager,name=IsrExpandsPerSec`: This specifies the rate at which in-sync replicas expand. It can give these values as a mean, minute rate, 5 minute rate, and 15 minute rate. It also gives the count of events.
- `kafka.server:type=ReplicaFetcherManager,name=MaxLag,clientId=Replica`: This specifies the maximum lag between the leader and the replicas.

See also

- Under the JConsole **MBean** tab we can see all the different Kafka MBeans available for monitoring

Monitoring producer statistics

As well as server metrics, there are also producer metrics.

Getting ready

For this recipe, we just need a Kafka broker up and running and JConsole installed.

How to do it...

1. Start the console producer for `test_topic` with the JMX parameters enabled with the following command:

   ```
   $ JMX_PORT=10102 bin/kafka-console-producer.sh --broker-list
   localhost:9092 --topic test_topic
   ```

2. Run JConsole using the following command:

   ```
   $ jconsole 127.0.0.1:10102
   ```

Chapter 9

3. In the following screenshot, see the **MBeans** tab with the Kafka producer metrics:

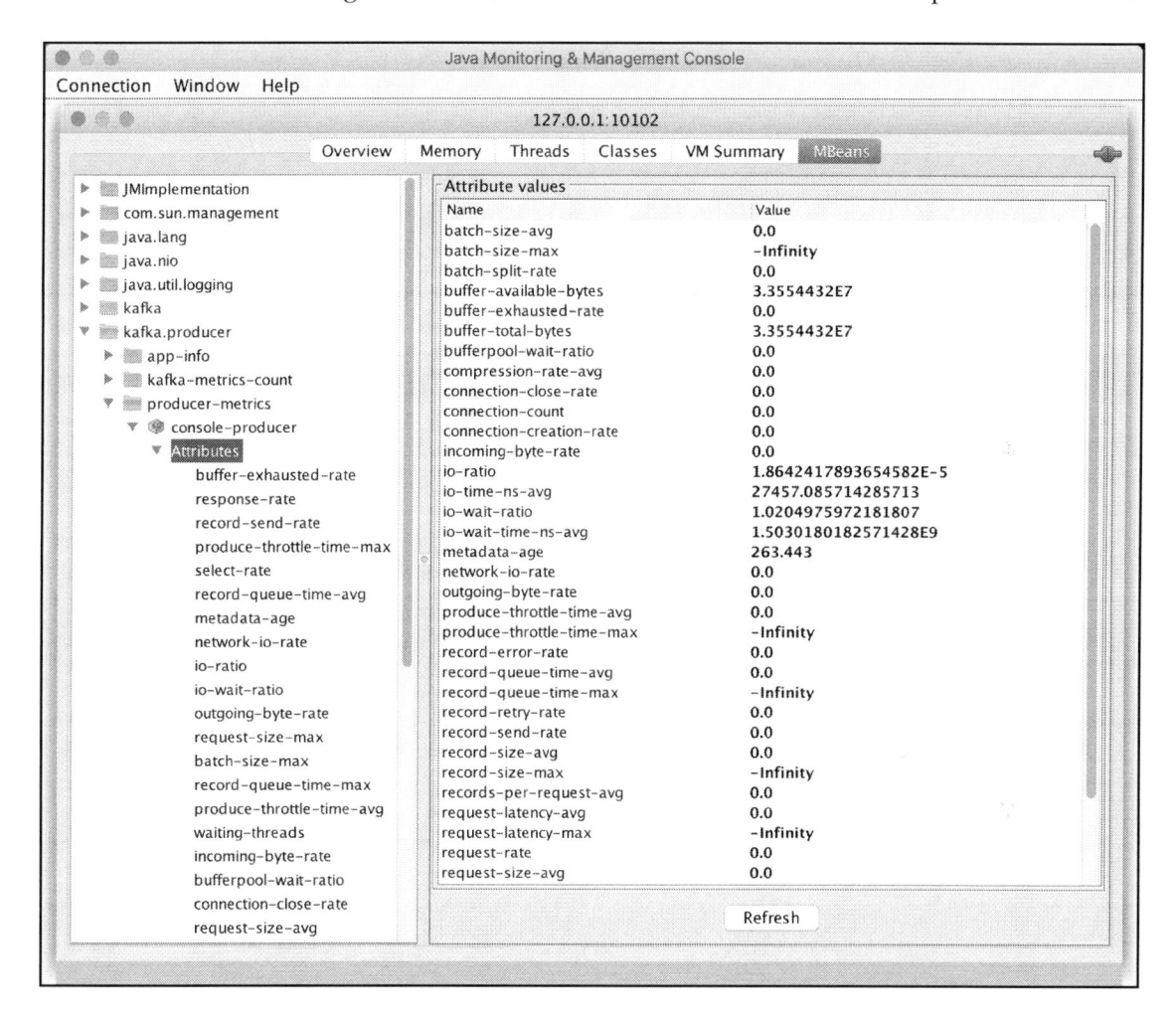

Figure 9.3: MBeans tab showing the Kafka producer metrics

How it works...

Switch to the **MBeans** tab in JConsole; there are several producer metrics. Some of them are as follows:

- `kafka.producer:type=ProducerRequestMetrics,name=ProducerRequest RateAndTimeMs,clientId=console-producer`: This gives values for the rate of producer requests taking place as the latencies involved. It gives latencies as a percentile: 50, 75, 95, 98, 99, and 99.9. It also gives the time to produce the data as a mean, minute average, 5 minute average, and 15 minute average. It also gives the count.
- `kafka.producer:type=ProducerRequestMetrics,name=ProducerRequest Size,clientId=console-producer`: This gives the request size for the producer. It gives: count, mean, max, min, standard deviation, and the request size percentile: 50, 75, 95, 98, 99, and 99.9.
- `kafka.producer:type=ProducerStats,name=FailedSendsPerSec,client Id=console-producer`: This gives the number of failed sends per second. It also gives the value of counts, the mean rate, minute average, 5 minute average, and 15 minute average value of the failed requests per second.
- `kafka.producer:type=ProducerStats,name=SerializationErrorsPerSe c,clientId=console-producer`: This gives the number of serialization errors per second. It also gives the value of counts, mean rate, minute average, 5 minute average, and 15 minute average value of the serialization errors per second.
- `kafka.producer:type=ProducerTopicMetrics,name=MessagesPerSec,cl ientId=console-producer`: This gives the number of messages produced per second. It also gives the value of counts, mean rate, minute average, 5 minute average, and 15 minute average of the messages produced per second.

See also

- More details of the producer metrics are available at: https://kafka.apache.org/documentation.html#monitoring

Monitoring consumer statistics

As well as producer metrics, there are also consumer metrics.

Getting ready

For this recipe, we just need a Kafka broker up and running and JConsole installed.

How to do it...

1. Start a console consumer for `test_topic` with the JMX parameters enabled:

   ```
   $ JMX_PORT=10103 bin/kafka-console-consumer.sh --bootstrap-server localhost:9092 --from-beginning --topic test_topic
   ```

2. Run JConsole using the following command:

   ```
   $ jconsole 127.0.0.1:10103
   ```

Monitoring and Security

3. In the following screenshot, see the **MBeans** tab with the Kafka consumer metrics:

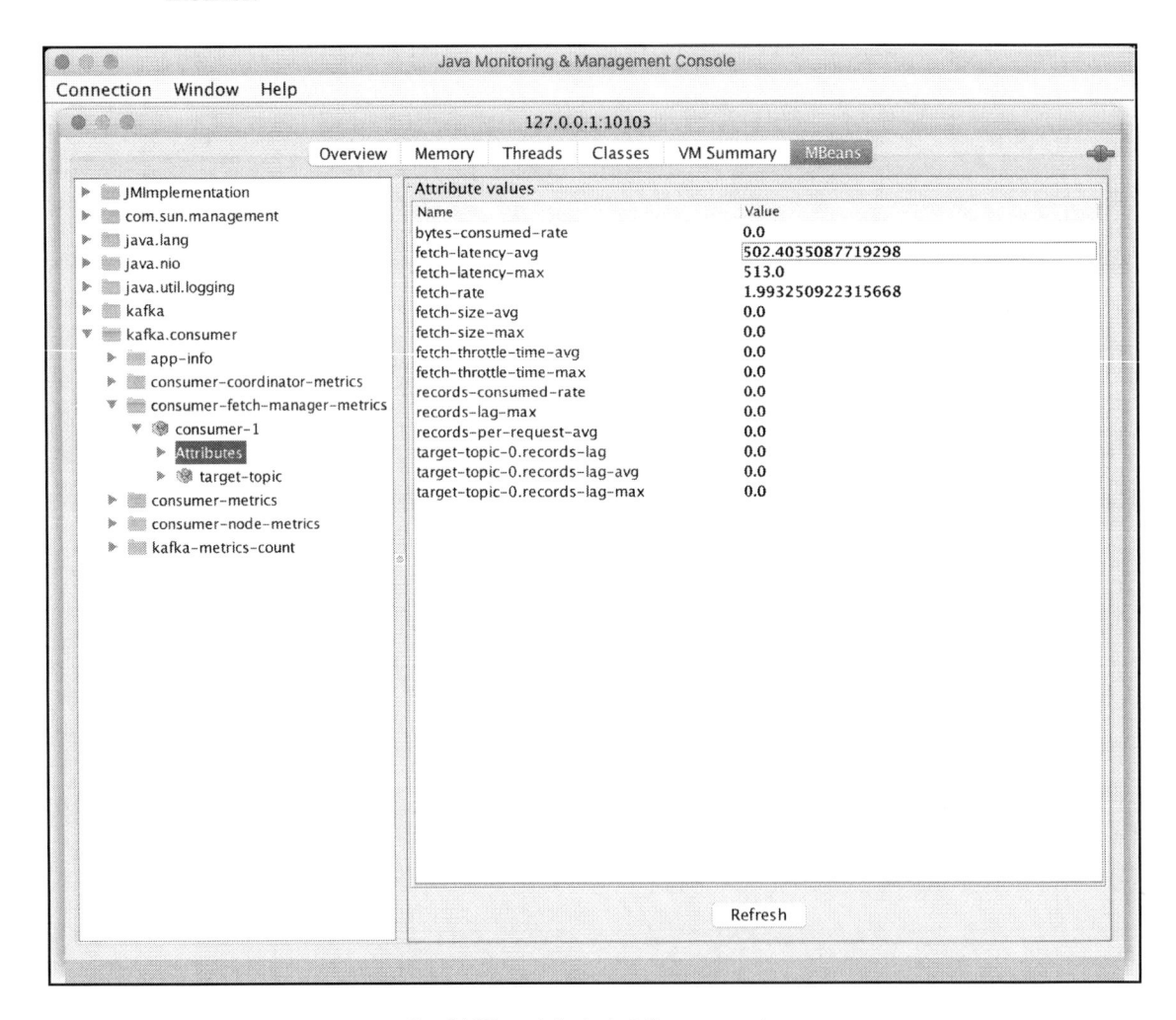

Figure 9.4: MBeans tab showing the Kafka consumer metrics

How it works...

Switch to the **MBeans** tab in JConsole; there are several consumer metrics. They are as follows:

- `kafka.consumer:type=ConsumerFetcherManager,name=MaxLag,clientId=test-consumer-group`: This tells us by how many messages the consumer is lagging behind the producer.
- `kafka.consumer:type=ConsumerFetcherManager,name=MinFetchRate,clientId=test-consumer-group`: This gives the minimum rate at which the consumer sends fetch requests to the broker. With a consumer dead, this value becomes close to zero.
- `kafka.consumer:type=ConsumerTopicMetrics,name=BytesPerSec,clientId=test-consumer-group`: This gives the number of bytes consumed per second. It gives values of count, mean rate, minute average, 5 minutes average, and 15 minutes average of the bytes consumed per second.
- `kafka.consumer:type=ConsumerTopicMetrics,name=MessagesPerSec,clientId=test-consumer-group`: This gives the number of messages consumed per second. It gives the value of count, mean rate, minute average, 5 minutes average, and 15 minutes average of the messages consumed per second.
- `kafka.consumer:type=FetchRequestAndResponseMetrics,name=FetchRequestRateAndTimeMs,clientId=test-consumer-group`: This gives values for the rate at which the consumer fetches the requests and the latencies involved in that process. It gives latency percentiles as: 50, 75, 95, 98, 99, and 99.9. It also gives the time taken to consume the data as a mean, minute rate, 5 minutes rate, and 15 minutes rate. It also gives the count.
- `kafka.consumer:type=FetchRequestAndResponseMetrics,name=FetchResponseSize,clientId=test-consumer-group`: This gives the fetch size for the consumer. It gives the count, mean, max, min, standard deviation, request size percentile: 50, 75, 95, 98, 99, and 99.9.
- `kafka.consumer:type=ZookeeperConsumerConnector,name=FetchQueueSize,clientId=test-consumer-group,topic=mytesttopic,threadId=0`: This gives the queue size for the fetch request for the client ID, thread ID, and topic requested.
- `kafka.consumer:type=ZookeeperConsumerConnector,name=KafkaCommitsPerSec,clientId=test-consumer-group`: This gives the fetch size for the Kafka commits per second. It gives the count, mean, minute average, 5 minutes average, and 15 minutes average rate of Kafka commits per second.

Monitoring and Security

- `kafka.consumer:type=ZookeeperConsumerConnector,name=RebalanceRateAndTime,clientId=test-consumer-group`: This gives the latency and rate of rebalance for the consumer. It gives latencies as latency percentiles: 50, 75, 95, 98, 99, and 99.9. It also gives the time taken to rebalance as a mean, minute rate, 5 minutes rate, and 15 minutes average. It also gives the count.
- `kafka.consumer:type=ZookeeperConsumerConnector,name=ZooKeeperCommitsPerSec,clientId=test-consumer-group`: This gives the fetch size for the ZooKeeper commits per second. It gives the count, mean, minute average, 5 minutes average, and 15 minutes average rate of ZooKeeper commits per second.

See also

- More details on consumer metrics are available at: `https://kafka.apache.org/documentation.html#monitoring`

Connecting with the help of Graphite

Graphite is a tool for diagnosing data systems in real time. Graphite has the ability to connect and get graphs of the system performance for a period of time. This recipe shows how to get system performance data from Kafka.

Getting ready

For this recipe, we just need a Kafka broker up and running and the Graphite server up and running.

How to do it...

1. Download the code for Kafka Graphite metrics reporter using the following link: `https://github.com/damienclaveau/kafka-Graphite/archive/master.zip`.
2. Unzip the file using the following command:

    ```
    $ unzip master.zip
    ```

3. Execute the Maven `clean package` command on the unzipped directory:

   ```
   $ mvn clean package
   ```

4. The previous command should have generated `kafka-Graphite-1.0.0.jar` in the `./target` directory.
5. In the `.m2/repository/com/yammer/metrics` Maven directory, this file should be generated: `/metrics-Graphite-2.2.0.jar`.
6. Copy both files to the `/libs` directory of the Kafka installation.
7. Add these lines to the `server.properties` file:

   ```
   kafka.metrics.reporters=com.criteo.kafka.kafkaGraphiteMetricsReporter
   kafka.graphite.metrics.reporter.enabled=true
   kafka.graphite.metrics.host=localhost
   kafka.graphite.metrics.port=8649
   kafka.graphite.metrics.group=kafka
   ```

8. Start the Kafka node. The Graphite system should start receiving the metrics from Kafka.
9. Create the Graphite graphs to monitor Kafka parameters as mentioned in the previous recipes.

How it works...

The first step downloads the code for Kafka Graphite metrics reporter. Next, Maven builds the package file for it.

By moving the two generated JAR files (`kafka-Graphite-1.0.0.jar` and `metrics-Graphite-2.2.0.jar`) to the `lib` directory, it allows Kafka to load them when it starts.

The entries in the `server.properties`:

- `kafka.metrics.reporters`: This tells Kafka the classes to load as metrics reporter. As mentioned in the first recipe of this chapter, Kafka makes use of Yammer metrics. One can have multiple metrics reports mentioned by listing their class names here in comma-separated form. For Kafka Graphite metrics reporter, the class to mention is: `com.criteo.kafka.KafkaGraphiteMetricsReporter`.

Monitoring and Security

- `kafka.Graphite.metrics.reporter.enabled`: This tells Kafka to enable Graphite metrics. If the value for this is true, the metrics are reported.
- `kafka.Graphite.metrics.host`: This the Graphite system hostname.
- `kafka.Graphite.metrics.port`: This the Graphite system port number.
- `kafka.Graphite.metrics.group`: This is the group name used to report metrics from this Kafka instance to Graphite.

See also

- The source code and more details on Kafka Graphite metrics reporter are available at: https://github.com/damienclaveau/kafka-graphite

Monitoring with the help of Ganglia

Ganglia is another important monitoring framework used to monitor Kafka. This recipe shows how to configure Kafka to report statistics in Ganglia.

Getting ready

Install Kafka on your machine.

How to do it...

1. Download the code for Kafka Ganglia metrics reporter using the following link: https://github.com/criteo/kafka-ganglia/archive/master.zip.
2. Unzip the file using the following command:

    ```
    $ unzip master.zip
    ```

3. Execute the Maven `clean package` command on the unzipped directory:

    ```
    $ mvn clean package
    ```

4. The previous command should have generated `kafka-ganglia-1.0.0.jar` in the `./target` directory.
5. In the `.m2/repository/com/yammer/metrics` Maven directory, this file should be generated: `/metrics-ganglia-2.2.0.jar`
6. Copy both files to the `/libs` directory of the Kafka installation.
7. Add these lines to the `server.properties` file:

   ```
   kafka.metrics.reporters=com.criteo.kafka.kafkaGangliaMetricsReporter
   kafka.ganglia.metrics.reporter.enabled=true
   kafka.ganglia.metrics.host=localhost
   kafka.ganglia.metrics.port=8649
   kafka.ganglia.metrics.group=kafka
   ```

8. Start the Kafka node. The Ganglia reporter system should start receiving the metrics from Kafka.
9. Create the Ganglia dashboard to monitor the Kafka metrics. Next, you have to start the Kafka node on that machine.

How it works...

The first step downloads the code for the Kafka Ganglia reporter system. Next, Maven builds the package file for it.

By moving the two generated JAR files (`kafka-ganglia-1.0.0.jar` and `metrics-ganglia-2.2.0.jar`) to the `lib` directory, it allows Kafka to load them when it starts.

The entries in the `server.properties`:

- `kafka.metrics.reporters`: This tells Kafka which classes to load in the metrics reporter. As mentioned in the first recipe of this chapter, Kafka makes use of Yammer metrics. One can have multiple metrics reports mentioned by listing their class names here in comma-separated form. For Kafka Ganglia metrics reporter, the class to mention is `com.criteo.kafka.KafkaGangliaMetricsReporter`.
- `kafka.ganglia.metrics.reporter.enabled` tells Kafka to enable Ganglia metrics. If the value for this is true, the metrics are reported.

- `kafka.ganglia.metrics.host`: This the Ganglia system hostname.
- `kafka.ganglia.metrics.port`: This is the Ganglia system port number.
- `kafka.ganglia.metrics.group`: This the group name used to report metrics from this Kafka instance to Ganglia.

See also

- The source code and more details on Kafka Ganglia metrics reporter are available at: https://github.com/criteo/kafka-ganglia
- Other JMX reporters available for Kafka are mentioned at this link: https://cwiki.apache.org/confluence/display/KAFKA/JMX+Reporters

Implementing authentication using SSL

The communication between clients and brokers is allowed over SSL using a dedicated port. This port is not enabled by default. This recipe shows how to enable encryption using SSL.

How to do it...

1. Use the Java `keytool` to generate an SSL key on each machine with the following command:

   ```
   keytool -keystore kafka.server.keystore.jks -alias localhost -validity {validity} -genkey
   ```

   For this command, `validity` is the valid time of the certificate in days.

2. To create your own **Certificate Authority** (**CA**), run the following command:

   ```
   openssl req -new -x509 -keyout ca-key -out ca-cert -days {validity}
   ```

Chapter 9

3. To add the generated CA to the clients' trust store, run the following command:

   ```
   keytool -keystore kafka.client.truststore.jks -alias CARoot -import
   -file ca-cert
   ```

4. To sign the certificates in the keystore with the CA we generated, export the certificate from the keystore as follows:

   ```
   keytool -keystore kafka.server.keystore.jks -alias localhost -
   certreq -file cert-file
   ```

5. Sign it with the CA:

   ```
   openssl x509 -req -CA ca-cert -CAkey ca-key -in cert-file -out
   cert-signed -days {validity} -CAcreateserial -passin pass:{ca-
   password}
   ```

6. Import both the certificate of the CA and the signed certificate into the keystore:

   ```
   keytool -keystore kafka.server.keystore.jks -alias CARoot -import -
   file ca-cert
   keytool -keystore kafka.server.keystore.jks -alias localhost -
   import -file cert-signed
   ```

7. The following SSL configurations are needed for the broker configuration:

   ```
   ssl.keystore.location=/var/private/ssl/kafka.server.keystore.jks
   ssl.keystore.password=your_keystore_password
   ssl.key.password=your_key_password
   ssl.truststore.location=/var/private/ssl/kafka.server.truststore.jk
   s
   ssl.truststore.password=your_truststore_password
   ```

8. To enable SSL for inter-broker communication, change the following line in the broker properties file:

   ```
   security.inter.broker.protocol = SSL
   ```

9. If client authentication is not required by the broker, the following is the configuration:

   ```
   security.protocol=SSL
   ssl.truststore.location=/var/private/ssl/kafka.client.truststore.jk
   s
   ssl.truststore.password=your_truststore_password
   ssl.keystore.location=/var/private/ssl/kafka.client.keystore.jks
   ```

```
ssl.keystore.password=your_keystore_password
ssl.key.password=your_key_password
```

10. Finally, to enable SSL logging, add the following line in the `bin/kafka-run-class.sh` file:

    ```
    -Djavax.net.debug=all
    ```

    Add the preceding line in the following section:

    ```
    if [ -z "$KAFKA_JMX_OPTS" ]; then
    KAFKA_JMX_OPTS="add here" -Dcom.sun.management.jmxremote -Dcom.sun.management.jmxremote.authenticate=false -Dcom.sun.management.jmxremote.ssl=false "
    fi
    ```

See also

- The official documentation for SSL authentication is at: https://docs.confluent.io/current/kafka/ssl.html

Implementing authentication using SASL/Kerberos

Currently, the supported mechanisms are **Generic Security Services API (GSSAPI)** or Kerberos and PLAIN.

How to do it...

To configure SASL authentication on the brokers perform the following:

1. Select one or more mechanisms to enable in the broker: GSSAPI or PLAIN
2. Add the JAAS config file location as a JVM parameter to each Kafka broker:

   ```
   -Djava.security.auth.login.config=/etc/kafka/kafka_server_jaas.conf
   ```

3. Configure an SASL port in `server.properties` by adding at least one of `SASL_PLAINTEXT` or `SASL_SSL` to the listeners, and optionally, `advertised.listeners` properties, each of which should contain one or more comma-separated values:

   ```
   listeners=SASL_PLAINTEXT://host.name:port
   advertised.listeners=SASL_PLAINTEXT://host.name:port
   security.inter.broker.protocol=SASL_PLAINTEXT (or SASL_SSL)
   ```

4. Enable one or more SASL mechanisms in `server.properties` and configure the SASL mechanism for inter-broker communication if using SASL for inter-broker communication:

   ```
   sasl.enabled.mechanisms=GSSAPI,PLAIN
   sasl.mechanism.inter.broker.protocol=GSSAPI (or PLAIN)
   ```

To configure SASL authentication on the clients:

1. Select an SASL mechanism for authentication and add a JAAS config file for the selected mechanism, GSSAPI (Kerberos) or PLAIN
2. Add the JAAS config file location as a JVM parameter to each client JVM:

   ```
   -Djava.security.auth.login.config=/etc/kafka/kafka_client_jaas.conf
   ```

3. Configure the following properties in `producer.properties` or `consumer.properties`:

   ```
   security.protocol=SASL_PLAINTEXT (or SASL_SSL)
   sasl.mechanism=GSSAPI (or PLAIN)
   ```

See also

- The official documentation for SASL authentication is at: https://docs.confluent.io/current/kafka/sasl.html

10
Third-Party Tool Integration

This chapter covers the following topics: 1 x 1

- Moving data between Kafka nodes with Flume
- Writing to an HDFS cluster with Gobblin
- Moving data from Kafka to Elastic with Logstash
- Connecting Spark streams and Kafka
- Ingesting data from Kafka to Storm
- Pushing data from Kafka to Elastic
- Inserting data from Kafka to SolrCloud
- Building a Kafka producer with Akka
- Building a Kafka consumer with Akka
- Storing data in Cassandra
- Running Kafka on Mesos
- Reading Kafka with Apache Beam
- Writing to Kafka from Apache Beam

Introduction

As well as integration, this chapter also talks about real-time data processing tools and how to make a data processing pipeline with them. Tools such as Hadoop, Flume, Gobblin, Elastic, Logstash, Spark, Storm, Solr, Akka, Cassandra, Mesos, and Beam can read from and write to Kafka. Recently, the integration with Spark, Mesos, Akka, and Cassandra have transformed the reference stack for fast data processing.

Moving data between Kafka nodes with Flume

Apache Flume is a reliable, highly available, distributed service for collecting, aggregating, and moving large amounts of data logs into data storage solutions. The data storage destination might be HDFS, Kafka, Hive, or any of the various sinks that Flume supports.

Apache Flume can also be used to transfer data between Kafka nodes. The following recipe shows how to do that.

Getting ready

For this recipe, it is necessary to have two different Kafka brokers up and running, one to publish data (`source-topic`) and the other (`target-topic`) to receive data.

The installation of Apache Flume is also required. Follow the instructions on this page: https://flume.apache.org/download.html.

How to do it...

1. In the `conf` folder, create a Flume configuration file called `flume.conf` with this content:

   ```
   flume1.sources = kafka-source-1
   flume1.channels = mem-channel-1
   flume1.sinks = kafka-sink-1

   flume1.sources.kafka-source-1.type=org.apache.flume.source.kafka.KafkaSource
   flume1.sources.kafka-source-1.zookeeperConnect = localhost:2181
   flume1.sources.kafka-source-1.topic = source-topic
   flume1.sources.kafka-source-1.batchSize = 100
   flume1.sources.kafka-source-1.channels = mem-channel-1

   flume1.channels.mem-channel-1.type = memory

   flume1.sinks.kafka-sink-1.type = org.apache.flume.sink.kafka.KafkaSink
   flume1.sinks.kafka-sink-1.brokerList = localhost:9092
   flume1.sinks.kafka-sink-1.topic = target-topic
   ```

```
flume1.sinks.kafka-sink-1.batchSize = 50
flume1.sinks.kafka-sink-1.channel = mem-channel-1
```

2. With this configuration file, start the Flume agent to start consuming data from `source-topic` and push the data to the `target-topic` with the following command (make sure the Flume bin folder is set in the PATH env variable):

```
$ flume-ng agent --conf-file flume.conf --name flume1
```

How it works...

In this context, Flume has three actors: a source where the data is extracted (here called `source-1`), a sink in Flume where the data is written (here called `sink-1`), and the channel (here called `channel-1`), which passes data between source and sink.

First, declare `flume1` as a Flume instance. The first three lines declare the names of the source (`source-1`), channel (`channel-1`), and sink (`sink-1`).

The following five lines declare the configuration of the source:

- `org.apache.flume.source.kafka.KafkaSource`: This is the source type.
- `zookeeperConnect`: This specifies the ZooKeeper connection string, a comma-separated list in the format `host:port`.
- `topic`: This specifies the topic which the source will read from. At the time of writing, Flume supports only one Kafka topic per source.
- `batchSize`: This specifies the maximum number of messages at each time that might be fetched from Kafka and written into a channel. The default value is `1000`. This value is determined by the amount of data the channel can process in one fetch.
- `batchDurationMillis`: This specifies the maximum time in milliseconds the system will wait before writing the batch into the channel. If `batchSize` is exceeded before this time, the batch will be written to the channel. The default value is `1000`.

The following line defines the channel between the source and sink. In this example, memory is used to hold the data, so it is a memory channel. The following values are used to configure a channel:

- `type`: This is set as `memory` to indicate the use of the memory channel. A channel could be of type memory, JDBC, file, or Kafka channel (without buffering).
- `capacity`: This is the maximum number of messages stored in memory. Declare it based on the memory capacity and message size. Its default value is `100`.
- `transactionCapacity`: This is the maximum number of messages to take from the source or sink in a single transaction.

The following five lines declare the sink settings:

- `org.apache.flume.sink.kafka.KafkaSink`: This the first line that declares the sink type.
- `brokerList`: This specifies the list of Kafka cluster brokers to write the messages. The broker address is a comma-separated list in the format `host:port`.
- `topic`: This specifies the Kafka topic to write the messages.
- `batchSize`: This specifies the number of messages to write at one time.
- `channel`: This declares the name of the channel from which we collect the data.

See also

- More information on Apache Flume can be found in the user guide at: `https://flume.apache.org/FlumeUserGuide.html`

Writing to an HDFS cluster with Gobblin

Gobblin is a universal data ingestion framework for the **extract, transform, and load** (ETL) of large volumes of data from a variety of data sources, such as files, databases, and Hadoop.

Gobblin also performs regular data ETL operations, such as job/task scheduling, state management, task partitioning, error handling, data quality checking, and data publishing.

Some features that make Gobblin very attractive are auto scalability, extensibility, fault tolerance, data quality assurance, and the ability to handle data model evolution.

Getting ready

For this recipe, it is necessary to have a Kafka cluster up and running. We also need an HDFS cluster up and running, into which we write the data.

The installation of Gobblin is also required. Follow the instructions on this page: http://gobblin.readthedocs.io/en/latest/Getting-Started.

How to do it...

1. Edit a file called `kafkagobblin.conf` with the following contents; the instructions to read from Kafka and write into HDFS:

   ```
   job.name=KafkaGobblinTest
   job.group=kafkaGoblinGroup
   job.description=Kafka Gobblin connection
   job.lock.enabled=false

   source.class=gobblin.source.extractor.extract.kafka.KafkaAvroSource
   extract.namespace=gobblin.extract.kafka

   writer.destination.type=HDFS
   writer.output.format=AVRO
   writer.fs.uri=file://localhost/
   writer.partition.level=hourly
   writer.partition.pattern=YYYY/MM/dd/HH
   writer.builder.class=gobblin.writer.AvroTimePartitionedWriterBuilder
   writer.file.path.type=tablename
   writer.partition.column.name=header.time

   data.publisher.type=gobblin.publisher.TimePartitionedDataPublisher

   topic.whitelist=source-topic
   bootstrap.with.offset=earliest

   kafka.brokers=localhost:2181
   mr.job.max.mappers=20

   extract.limit.enabled=true
   extract.limit.type=time
   extract.limit.time.limit=15
   extract.limit.time.limit.timeunit=minutes
   ```

2. Start Gobblin as follows:

```
$ gobblin-standalone.sh start --workdir gobblinWorkDir --conffile kafkagobblin.conf
```

How it works...

The configuration file tells Gobblin how to create the Gobblin job.

The first three lines declare the job metadata:

- `job.name`: This specifies the job name
- `job.group`: This specifies the job group name
- `job.description`: This gives the job a description

The following line declares the class to use as the data source, `source.class`:

- If Kafka and the Avro file format is used, set the type to: `gobblin.source.extractor.extract.Kafka.KafkaAvroSource`
- If Kafka is used but not the Avro format, set the type to: `gobblin.source.extractor.extract.Kafka.KafkaSimpleSources`

There are other types of source classes. See the Gobblin GitHub repository at: `https://github.com/apache/incubator-gobblin/tree/master/gobblin-core/src/main/java/org/apache/gobblin/source/extractor/extract`:

- `extract.namespace`: This specifies that the namespace for the extracted data will be a part of the default filename of the data written out

The following lines specify the writer properties:

- `writer.destination.type`: This specifies the destination type for the writer task. At the time of writing only HDFS is supported.
- `writer.output.format`: This specifies the output format. At the time of writing only the Avro format is supported.
- `writer.fs.uri`: This specifies the URI of the file system to write into.
- `writer.partition.level`: This specifies the partitioning level for the writer. The default value is `daily`.

- `writer.partition.pattern`: This specifies the pattern for partitioning the written data.
- `writer.builder.class`: This is the class name of the writer builder.
- `writer.file.path.type`: This is the file path type, in this case `tablename`.
- `writer.partition.column.name`: This is the column name of the partition.

Some other properties are as follows:

- `data.publisher.type`: This is the name of the `DataPublisher` class that will publish the task data once everything has been completed
- `topic.whitelist`: This is the white list of topics from which data is read
- `bootstrap.with.offset`: This is the property in which offset Gobblin will start reading the Kafka data
- `kafka.brokers`: This is the comma-separated Kafka brokers to read data from
- `mr.job.max.mappers`: This is used to specify the number of tasks to launch
- `extract.limit.enabled`: If this is true, the extract task specifies a limit
- `extract.limit.type`: This is the type of limit, by time, rate, count, or pool
- `extract.limit.time.limit`: This specifies the limit on the tasks
- `extract.limit.time.limit.timeunit`: This specifies the units to be used for the limit

See also

- More information on Gobblin is available at: http://gobblin.readthedocs.io/en/latest/

Moving data from Kafka to Elastic with Logstash

Logstash is a tool from Elastic (http://www.elastic.co/). Logstash simplifies log extraction from any source with Elasticsearch. It also allows centralizing data processing and normalizing schemas and formats for several data types. This recipe shows how to read with Logstash from Kafka and push the data to Elastic.

Getting ready

Have a Kafka cluster up and running. To install Elasticsearch follow the instructions on this page: `https://www.elastic.co/guide/en/elasticsearch/reference/current/_installation.html`.

To install Logstash follow the instructions on this page: `https://www.elastic.co/guide/en/logstash/current/installing-logstash.html`.

How to do it...

To read data from Kafka and write it into Elasticsearch with Logstash:

1. Write a file named `kafkalogstash.conf` with this content:

```
input {
    kafka {
        bootstrap_servers => "localhost:9092"
        topics => ["source-topic"]
    }
}
output {
    elasticsearch {
        host => localhost
    }
}
```

2. Start Logstash with the following command.

```
$ bin/logstash -f kafkalogstash.conf
```

How it works...

The config file defines the input and output for Logstash. For input, Kafka is used; for output, Elasticsearch.

Some of the properties of the configuration file are:

- `bootstrap_servers`: The brokers to connect to, in the `host:port` format.
- `topics`: This is an array of source topics that is read from.

- `client_id`: This is the consumer ID to be used when reading from Kafka. If it is not specified it is automatically generated.
- `group_id`: This is the group ID to be used by the Logstash Kafka consumer. If it is not specified it is set to `logstash`.
- `fetch_max_bytes`: This is the maximum number of bytes fetched from the Kafka topic in each fetch request. It helps to control the memory used by Logstash while storing the message.

There's more...

The Kafka input plugin for Logstash has more interesting settings. For more info visit: https://www.elastic.co/guide/en/logstash/current/plugins-inputs-kafka.html.

See also

- There is a Kafka output plugin for Logstash. For more info visit: https://www.elastic.co/guide/en/logstash/current/plugins-outputs-kafka.html

Connecting Spark streams and Kafka

Apache Spark is an open source computer framework. Spark's in-memory processing performs up to 100 times faster for certain traditional applications. It is used for making distributed real-time data analytics. Spark has very good integration with Kafka for reading and writing data processed by Kafka.

Getting ready

For this recipe a running Kafka cluster is needed. To install Apache Spark follow the instructions on this page: https://spark.apache.org/downloads.html.

How to do it...

Spark has a simple utility class to create the data stream to be read from Kafka.

1. The first thing in any Spark project is to create Spark configuration and the Spark streaming context:

   ```
   SparkConf sparkConf = new SparkConf().setAppName("KafkaSparkTest");
   JavaStreamingContext jssc =
       new JavaStreamingContext(sparkConf, Durations.seconds(10));
   ```

2. Then, create the `HashSet` for the topic and the Kafka consumer parameters:

   ```
   HashSet<String> topicsSet = new HashSet<String>();
   topicsSet.add("source-topic");
   HashMap<String, String> kafkaParams = new HashMap<String, String>();
   kafkaParams.put("metadata.broker.list", "localhost:9092");
   ```

3. Create a direct Kafka stream with brokers and topics:

   ```
   JavaPairInputDStream<String, String> messages =
   KafkaUtils.createDirectStream(
           jssc,
           String.class,
           String.class,
           StringDecoder.class,
           StringDecoder.class,
           kafkaParams,
           topicsSet
       );
   ```

4. With this stream, run the Spark data processing.

How it works...

In the second line, the Java streaming context is created that sets up the input for all the processing functionality; the duration of the batch interval is set to 10 seconds.

In the next line, a HashSet is created to read from the Kafka topic.

The next line sets the parameters for the Kafka producer using a HashMap. This map has a value for `metadata.broker.list`, which is a comma-separated list in the format `host:port`.

Finally, the input `DStream` is created using the `KafkaUtils` class.

When the `DStream` is ready, the data algorithms can be applied.

There's more...

The Apache Spark programming guide is available at: http://spark.apache.org/docs/latest/streaming-programming-guide.html.

Ingesting data from Kafka to Storm

Apache Storm is a real-time, distributed stream-processing system. Storm simplifies real-time data processing, Kafka can work as the source for this data streaming.

Getting ready

Have a Kafka cluster up and running. To install Apache Storm follow the instructions on this page: http://storm.apache.org/downloads.html.

How to do it...

Storm has a built-in `KafkaSpout` to easily ingest data from Kafka to the Storm topology:

1. The first step is to create the `ZkHosts` object with the ZooKeeper address in `host:port` format:

   ```
   BrokerHosts hosts = new ZkHosts("127.0.0.1:2181");
   ```

2. Next, create the `SpoutConfig` object that contains the parameters needed for `KafkaSpout`:

   ```
   SpoutConfig kafkaConf = new SpoutConfig(hosts,"source-topic",
   "/brokers", "kafkaStormTest");
   ```

3. Then, declare the scheme for the `KafkaSpout` config:

   ```
   kafkaConf.scheme = new SchemeAsMultiScheme(new StringScheme());
   ```

4. Using this scheme, create a `KafkaSpout` object:

   ```
   KafkaSpout kafkaSpout = new KafkaSpout(kafkaConf);
   ```

5. Build that topology with this `KafkaSpout` and run it:

   ```
   TopologyBuilder builder = new TopologyBuilder();
   builder.setSpout("spout", kafkaSpout, 10);
   ```

6. After this, connect some Storm bolts to process the data.

How it works...

1. The first step is to create the `ZkHosts` object with the ZooKeeper address in a comma-separated list in the format `host:port`.
2. Initialize the `SpoutConfig` object. This configuration object takes the `ZkHosts` object, the Kafka topic to obtain the data, the root directory in ZooKeeper (where topics and partition information is stored), and a unique spout identifier.
3. Create a new `SpoutConfig` scheme.
4. Create the `KafkaSpout` object. This is needed to initialize the Storm topology.
5. To build a Storm topology, a `TopologyBuilder` class object is instantiated.
6. Set the spout for the `TopologyBuilder` using the function `setSpout`, which takes the spout name, the spout object, and the parallelism hint as input.
7. The parallelism hint is the number of threads created for the spout. This should be a multiple of the existing Kafka partitions (in this case `10`).

There's more...

The Storm Javadoc contains more information about the configurations for the Kafka consumer.

At the time of writing, this is the latest version: `http://storm.apache.org/releases/1.1.1/javadocs/index.html`.

See also

- For more information on Storm, visit the home page: http://storm.apache.org/releases/1.1.1/index.html

Pushing data from Kafka to Elastic

As mentioned, Elasticsearch is a distributed, full-text search engine that supports a RESTful web interface and schema-free JSON documents. Elasticsearch was built with distributed searches in mind. There are several ways to push data into Elasticsearch. In this recipe, the plugin that enables data pushing from Kafka to Elasticsearch is analyzed.

Getting ready

For this recipe, a Kafka cluster must be up and running and a confluent platform is needed. To install Elasticsearch follow the instructions on this page: https://www.elastic.co/guide/en/elasticsearch/reference/current/_installation.html.

How to do it...

The Elasticsearch connector is needed. Before starting the connector, the configuration is in etc/kafka-connect-elasticsearch/quickstart-elasticsearch.properties.

This must be properly set to the Elasticsearch configuration: connection.url points to the correct HTTP address.

To start the Elasticsearch connector, use the following command:

```
$ ./bin/connect-standalone etc/schema-registry/connect-avro-standalone.properties \
etc/kafka-connect-elasticsearch/quickstart-elasticsearch.properties

$ confluent load elasticsearch-sink
{
  "name": "elasticsearch-sink",
  "config": {
    "connector.class":
"io.confluent.connect.elasticsearch.ElasticsearchSinkConnector",
    "tasks.max": "1",
```

```
    "topics": "topic-elastic-sink",
    "key.ignore": "true",
    "connection.url": "http://localhost:9200",
    "type.name": "kafka-connect",
    "name": "elasticsearch-sink"
  },
  "tasks": []
}
```

How it works...

To check that the data is available in Elasticsearch, we perform the following:

```
$ curl -XGET 'http://localhost:9200/topic-elastic-sink/_search?pretty'
{
 "took" : 2,
 "timed_out" : false,
 "_shards" : {
   "total" : 5,
   "successful" : 5,
   "failed" : 0
 },
 "hits" : {
   "total" : 1,
   "max_score" : 1.0,
   "hits" : [ {
     "_index" : "topic-elastic-sink",
     "_type" : "kafka-connect",
     "_id" : "test-elasticsearch-sink+0+0",
     "_score" : 1.0,
     "_source" : {
       "f1" : "value1"
     }
   } ]
 }
}
```

See also

- Check the confluent's Elasticsearch Kafka connector page at: https://docs.confluent.io/current/connect/connect-elasticsearch/docs/elasticsearch_connector.html

Inserting data from Kafka to SolrCloud

Solr is a highly-available, fault-tolerant environment for distributing indexed content and query requests across multiple servers. It is not possible to insert data into Solr directly; a tool like Flume is needed.

Getting ready

For this recipe a Kafka cluster must be up and running.

To install Solr follow the instructions on this page: `https://lucene.apache.org/solr/guide/6_6/installing-solr.html`.

The installation of Apache Flume is also required, follow the instructions on this page: `https://flume.apache.org/download.html`.

How to do it...

1. Create a Flume configuration file called `flume.conf` with this content:

    ```
    flume1.sources = kafka-source-1
    flume1.channels = mem-channel-1
    flume1.sinks = solr-sink-1

    flume1.sources.kafka-source-1.type=org.apache.flume.source.kafka.KafkaSource
    flume1.sources.kafka-source-1.zookeeperConnect = localhost:2181
    flume1.sources.kafka-source-1.topic = source-topic
    flume1.sources.kafka-source-1.batchSize = 100
    flume1.sources.kafka-source-1.channels = mem-channel-1

    flume1.channels.mem-channel-1.type = memory

    flume1.sinks.solr-sink-1.type=org.apache.flume.sink.solr.morphline.MorphlineSolrSink
    flume1.sinks.solr-sink-1.brokerList = localhost:9092
    flume1.sinks.solr-sink-1.batchSize = 100
    flume1.sinks.solr-sink-1.channel = mem-channel-1

    flume1.sinks.solr-sink-1.batchDurationMillis = 1000
    flume1.sinks.solr-sink-1.morphlineFile = /etc/flume-ng/conf/morphline.conf
    ```

```
            flume1.sinks.solr-sink-1.morphlineId = morphline1
```

2. Run Flume using the configuration file created:

   ```
   $ flume-ng agent --conf-file flume.conf --name flume1
   ```

How it works...

The Kafka configurations are the same as those used in the first recipe of this chapter with some changes.

The Solr sink has the following characteristics:

- `type`: This is the Solr type and is defined as `org.apache.flume.sink.solr.morphline.MorphlineSolrSink`
- `batchSize`: This specifies the number of messages processed in one fetch
- `batchDurationMillis`: If the number of messages to be processed crosses the batch size number, this number specifies the milliseconds to wait till all the messages are processed
- `morphlineFile`: This specifies the path to the `morphline` configuration file
- `morphlineId` This is the identifier for the `morphline` configuration file if the configuration file has multiple files

See also

- More information on Apache Flume is in the Flume user guide at: `https://flume.apache.org/FlumeUserGuide.html`.

Building a Kafka producer with Akka

According to the definition, Akka is a free and open source toolkit and runtime that simplifies the construction of concurrent and distributed applications for the JVM. There is a big infrastructure for connecting both projects.

In this recipe, a Kafka producer is built with Akka.

Getting ready

The Akka connector is available at Maven Central for Scala 2.11 at the following Maven coordinates:

```
libraryDependencies += "com.typesafe.akka" %% "akka-stream-kafka" % "0.11-M4"
```

How to do it...

A producer publishes messages to Kafka topics. The message itself contains information about what topic and partition to publish. One can publish to different topics with the same producer. The underlying implementation uses the Kafka producer.

When creating a producer stream, specify the `ProducerSettings` defining the following:

- Kafka cluster bootstrap server
- Serializers for the keys and values
- Tuning parameters

The imports necessary for `ProducerSettings` are as follows:

```
import akka.kafka._
import akka.kafka.scaladsl._
import org.apache.kafka.common.serialization.StringSerializer
import org.apache.kafka.common.serialization.ByteArraySerializer
```

To declare and define the `ProducerSettings`:

```
val producerSettings = ProducerSettings(system, new ByteArraySerializer,
new StringSerializer).withBootstrapServers("localhost:9092")
```

The easiest way to publish messages is through `Producer.plainSink`. The sink consumes `ProducerRecord` elements, which contain a topic name to send the messages, an optional partition number, and an optional key and value.

How it works...

For example, to produce 10,000 messages we perform the following:

```
Source(1 to 10000)
  .map(_.toString)
  .map(elem => new ProducerRecord[Array[Byte], String]("sink-topic", elem))
  .to(Producer.plainSink(producerSettings))
```

There's more...

To produce the same 10,000 messages but using `flow`, we perform the following:

```
Source(1 to 10000).map(elem => ProducerMessage.Message(new
ProducerRecord[Array[Byte], String]("sink-topic", elem.toString), elem))
    .via(Producer.flow(producerSettings))
    .map { result =>
      val record = result.message.record
      println(s"${record.topic}/${record.partition} ${result.offset}:
${record.value} (${result.message.passThrough}")
      result
    }
```

Building a Kafka consumer with Akka

In this recipe, a Kafka consumer is built with Akka.

Getting ready

The Akka connector is available at Maven Central for Scala 2.11 at the following Maven coordinates:

```
libraryDependencies += "com.typesafe.akka" %% "akka-stream-kafka" % "0.11-M4"
```

How to do it...

When creating a consumer stream, specify the `ProducerSettings` defining the following:

- Kafka cluster bootstrap server
- Serializers for the keys and values
- Tuning parameters

The imports necessary for `ConsumerSettings` are as follows:

```
import akka.kafka._
import akka.kafka.scaladsl._
import org.apache.kafka.common.serialization.StringDeserializer
import org.apache.kafka.common.serialization.ByteArrayDeserializer
import org.apache.kafka.clients.consumer.ConsumerConfig
```

To declare and define the `ConsumerSettings`:

```
val consumerSettings = ConsumerSettings(system, new ByteArrayDeserializer,
new StringDeserializer)
  .withBootstrapServers("localhost:9092")
  .withGroupId("group1")
  .withProperty(ConsumerConfig.AUTO_OFFSET_RESET_CONFIG, "earliest")
```

This example consumes messages and stores a representation including the offset:

```
db.loadOffset().foreach {
   fromOffset => val subscription =
        Subscriptions.assignmentWithOffset(
            new TopicPartition("source-topic", 1) -> fromOffset)
        Consumer.plainSource(consumerSettings, subscription)
        .mapAsync(1)(db.save)
}
```

This example consumes messages in at-most-once form:

```
Consumer.atMostOnceSource(consumerSettings.withClientId("client-1"),
Subscriptions.topics("source-topic"))
    .mapAsync(1) { record =>
      rocket.launch(record.value)
}
```

Third-Party Tool Integration

This example consumes messages in at-least-once form:

```
Consumer.committableSource(consumerSettings.withClientId("client-1"),
Subscriptions.topics("source-topic"))
    .mapAsync(1) {
      msg => db.update(msg.value).flatMap(_ =>
        msg.committableOffset.commitScaladsl())
}
```

This example connects the consumer with the producer in the previous recipe:

```
Consumer.committableSource(consumerSettings.withClientId("client-1"))
    .map(msg => ProducerMessage.Message(
        new ProducerRecord[Array[Byte], String]("source-topic", msg.value),
          msg.committableOffset))
    .to(Producer.commitableSink(producerSettings))
```

This example consumes messages in at-least-once form, and commits in batches:

```
Consumer.committableSource(consumerSettings.withClientId("client-1"),
Subscriptions.topics("source-topic"))
    .mapAsync(1) { msg =>
      db.update(msg.value).map(_ => msg.committableOffset)
    }
    .batch(max = 10, first =>
        CommittableOffsetBatch.empty.updated(first)) { (batch, elem) =>
          batch.updated(elem)
    }.mapAsync(1)(_.commitScaladsl())
```

How to make a Kafka consumer Akka actor:

```
val consumer:
    ActorRef = system.actorOf(KafkaConsumerActor.props(consumerSettings))
```

This example assigns two topic partitions to the consumer manually:

```
val streamP1 = Consumer
    .plainExternalSource[Array[Byte], String](consumer,
Subscriptions.assignment(new TopicPartition("source-topic", 1)))
    .via(business)
    .to(Sink.ignore)

val streamP2 = Consumer
    .plainExternalSource[Array[Byte], String](consumer,
Subscriptions.assignment(new TopicPartition("source-topic", 2)))
    .via(business)
    .to(Sink.ignore)
```

This example uses a consumer group:

```
val consumerGroup = Consumer.committablePartitionedSource(
  consumerSettings.withClientId("client-1"),
  Subscriptions.topics("source-topic"))
consumerGroup.map {
  case (topicPartition, source) =>
    source
      .via(business)
      .toMat(Sink.ignore)(Keep.both)
      .run()
}.mapAsyncUnordered(maxPartitions)(_._2)
```

Storing data in Cassandra

According to the definition, Apache Cassandra is a free and open source, distributed NoSQL database management system designed to handle large amounts of data across many commodity servers, providing high availability with no single point of failure. This recipe shows how to connect Kafka and Cassandra.

Getting ready

This recipe uses a Kafka-Cassandra connector published on Maven Central by Tuplejump.

It can be defined as a dependency in the build file. For example, with SBT:

```
libraryDependencies += "com.tuplejump" %% "kafka-connect-cassandra" % "0.0.7"
```

How to do it...

Data can be fetched from Cassandra in two modes:

- Bulk
- Timestamp-based

The modes change automatically based on the query. For example, bulk:

```
SELECT * FROM userlog;
```

For example, timestamp-based:

```
SELECT * FROM userlog WHERE ts > previousTime();
SELECT * FROM userlog WHERE ts = currentTime();
SELECT * FROM userlog WHERE ts >= previousTime() AND ts <= currentTime() ;
```

How it works...

Cassandra sink stores Kafka sink records in Cassandra tables. At the time of writing, it only supports the STRUCT type in the sink record. The STRUCT can have multiple fields with primitive field types. Assume one-to-one mapping between the column names in the Cassandra sink table and the field names.

The sink records have this STRUCT value:

```
{    'id': 1,
     'username': 'Edward',
     'text': 'This is my first message'
}
```

The library doesn't create the Cassandra tables, the user must create them before starting the sink.

Running Kafka on Mesos

According to the definition, Apache Mesos is an open source project to manage computer clusters. This recipe shows how to run the Kafka on Mesos framework.

Getting ready

The following applications must be available on the machine:

- Java version 7 or later (http://openjdk.java.net/install/)
- Gradle (http://gradle.org/installation)

How to do it...

1. To download the Kafka on Mesos project from the repository, type the following command:

```
$ git clone https://github.com/mesos/kafka
$ cd kafka
$ ./gradlew jar
```

2. The following command downloads the Kafka executor:

```
$ wget https://archive.apache.org/dist/kafka/0.11.0.0/kafka_2.11-0.11.0.0.tgz
```

3. Set this environment variable pointing to the `libmesos.so` file:

```
$ export MESOS_NATIVE_JAVA_LIBRARY=/usr/local/lib/libmesos.so
```

4. Use the `kafka-mesos.sh` script to launch and configure Kafka on Mesos, but first create the `kafka-mesos.properties` file containing this:

```
storage=file:kafka-mesos.json
master=zk://master:2181/mesos
zk=master:2181
api=http://master:7000
```

These properties are used to configure `kafka-mesos.sh`, so we don't need to pass continuous arguments to the scheduler. The scheduler supports the following command-line arguments:

- `--api`: This is the API URL, for example `http://master:7000`.
- `--bind-address`: This is the scheduler bind address, for example: `master`, `0.0.0.0`, `192.168.50.*`, `if:eth1`). Default value: `all`.
- `--debug <Boolean>`: This is the debug mode. Default value: `false`.
- `--framework-name`: This is the framework name. Default value: `kafka`.
- `--framework-role`: This is the framework role. Default value: `*`.
- `--framework-timeout`: This is the framework timeout, for example: `30s`, `1m`, or `1h`. Default value: `30d`.

- `--jre`: This is the JRE ZIP file (`jre-7-openjdk.zip`). Default value: `none`.
- `--log`: This is the log file to use. Default value: `stdout`.
- `--master`: These are the master connection settings. Some examples are as follows:

    ```
    master:5050
    master:5050,master2:5050
    zk://master:2181/mesos
    zk://master:2181,master2:2181/mesos
    zk://username:password@master:2181
    ```

- `--principal`: This is the username used to register the framework. Default value: `none`.
- `--secret`: This is the password used to register the framework. Default value: `none`.
- `--storage`: This is the storage for the cluster state. Default value: `file:kafka-mesos.json`. Example values are as follows:

    ```
    file:kafka-mesos.json
    zk:/kafka-mesos
    ```

- `--user`: This is the Mesos user to run tasks. Default value: `none`.
- `--zk`: This is the Kafka ZooKeeper connect. For example:

    ```
    master:2181
    master:2181,master2:2181
    ```

How it works...

To start the Kafka scheduler, run the following command:

```
$ ./kafka-mesos.sh scheduler
```

To start the Kafka broker with the default settings, run the following command:

```
$ ./kafka-mesos.sh broker add 0
```

To check the brokers in the cluster, run the following command:

```
$ ./kafka-mesos.sh broker list
```

To start the broker, run the following command:

```
$ ./kafka-mesos.sh broker start 0
```

To test this setup, use the `kafkacat` command. To install the `kafkacat` run the following command:

```
$ sudo apt-get install kafkacat
$ echo "test" | kafkacat -P -b "10.213.128.5:31000" -t source-topic -p 0
```

To read the messages pushed to the broker with `kafkacat` use the following command:

```
$ kafkacat -C -b "10.213.128.5:31000" -t source-topic -p 0 -e test
```

To add more brokers to the cluster with just one command:

```
$ ./kafka-mesos.sh broker add 0..2 --heap 1024 --mem 2048
```

To start the three brokers added, run the following command:

```
$ ./kafka-mesos.sh broker start 0..2
```

To stop one broker, use the following command:

```
$ ./kafka-mesos.sh broker stop 0
```

To change the Kafka logs location of the stopped broker, use the following command:

```
$ ./kafka-mesos.sh broker update 0 --options log.dirs=/mnt/kafka/broker0
```

There's more...

To get the last 100 lines of the logs (`stdout`, `default`, and `stderr`) run the following command:

```
$ ./kafka-mesos.sh broker log 0
```

Use the following command to read from the `stderr` file:

```
$ ./kafka-mesos.sh broker log 0 --name stderr
```

To read a file in the `*/log/directory`, for example, the `server-1.log` file, use the following command:

```
$ ./kafka-mesos.sh broker log 0 --name server-1.log
```

To read a number of lines use the `--lines` option:

```
$ ./kafka-mesos.sh broker log 0 --name server.log --lines 200
```

Reading Kafka with Apache Beam

According to the definition, Apache Beam is an open source unified programming model to define and execute data processing pipelines, including ETL, batch, and stream processing. This recipe shows how to read Kafka with Apache Beam.

Getting ready

To install Apache Beam, follow the instructions at: https://beam.apache.org/get-started/quickstart-py/.

How to do it...

The following code shows how to write a Beam pipeline to read from Kafka. The example illustrates various options for configuring the Beam source:

```
pipeline
   .apply(KafkaIO.read()
        .withBootstrapServers("broker_1:9092,broker_2:9092")
        .withTopics(ImmutableList.of("topic_1", "topic_2"))

        .withKeyCoder(BigEndianLongCoder.of())
        .withValueCoder(StringUtf8Coder.of())
        .updateConsumerProperties(
            ImmutableMap.of("receive.buffer.bytes", 1024 * 1024))

      .withTimestampFn(new CustomTypestampFunction())
      .withWatermarkFn(new CustomWatermarkFunction())
      .withoutMetadata()
   )
   .apply(Values.<String>create())
```

How it works...

The `KafkaIO` returns an unbounded collection of Kafka records as `PCollection<KafkaRecord<K, V>>`. A Kafka record includes basic metadata such as topic, partition, and offset, with keys and values associated with a Kafka record.

Most applications consume a single topic. The source can be configured to consume multiple topics or even a specific set of topic partitions.

To configure a Kafka source, specify the Kafka bootstrap servers and one or more topics to consume.

There's more...

Kafka partitions are evenly distributed among splits (workers). Data flow check pointing is fully supported and each split can resume from the previous checkpoint.

When the pipeline starts for the first time without any checkpoint, the source starts consuming from the latest offsets. This behavior can be overridden to consume from the beginning, by setting appropriate properties in consumer configuration, through `KafkaIO.Read.updateConsumerProperties(Map)`.

See also

- Check the official Apache Beam documentation page at: https://beam.apache.org/documentation/sdks/javadoc/0.4.0/org/apache/beam/sdk/io/kafka/

Writing to Kafka from Apache Beam

This recipe shows how to write to Kafka with Apache Beam.

Getting ready

To install Apache Beam, follow the instructions at: `https://beam.apache.org/get-started/quickstart-py/`.

How to do it...

The following code shows how to write a Beam pipeline to write to Kafka. The example illustrates various options for configuring the Beam sink:

```
PCollection<KV<Long, String>> kvColl = ...;
kvColl.apply(KafkaIO.write()
    .withBootstrapServers("broker_1:9092, broker_2:9092")
    .withTopic("destination-topic")

    .withKeyCoder(BigEndianLongCoder.of())
    .withValueCoder(StringUtf8Coder.of())

    .updateProducerProperties(
      ImmutableMap.of("compression.type", "gzip"))
);
```

How it works...

The `KafkaIO` sink supports writing key value pairs to a Kafka topic. To configure a Kafka sink, specify the Kafka bootstrap servers and the topic to write to.

The `KafakIO` allows setting most of the properties in the consumer configuration for source, or in the producer configuration for sink. For example, to enable offset auto commit (for external monitoring), set `group.id`, `enable.auto.commit`, and so on.

There's more...

To only write values without any keys to Kafka, use `values()` to write records with the default `empty(null)` key:

```
PCollection<String> strings = ...;
strings.apply(KafkaIO.write()
    .withBootstrapServers("broker_1:9092, broker_2:9092")
    .withTopic("results")
    .withValueCoder(StringUtf8Coder.of())
    .values()
);
```

See also

- To read about the Apache Beam project go to: https://beam.apache.org

Index

A
aggregation 138
Akka
  Kafka consumer, building 210, 211, 212, 213
  Kafka producer, building 208
Apache Avro specification
  reference 61
Apache Beam project
  reference 221
Apache Beam
  Kafka, reading with 218, 219
  reference 218, 219
Apache Kafka download page
  reference 17
authentication
  implementing, SASL/Kerberos used 190, 191
  implementing, SSL used 188, 189

B
balancing leadership 163, 164
bit license 84
bit license regulatory framework
  reference 87
brew
  about 14
  reference 17
broker settings
  configuring 29, 30
broker
  about 10
  decommissioning 170, 171
  reference, for configurations 40

C
Cassandra
  data, storing in 213, 214
clusters
  about 10
  expanding 165, 167, 168
Confluent Cloud 114
Confluent Control Center
  about 114
  monitoring with 120, 121, 122, 123, 124
  reference 124
Confluent Enterprise v4.0 TAR files
  reference 116
Confluent open source v4.0
  download link 116
Confluent Platform open source
  components 114
Confluent Platform
  about 113
  enterprise, components 114
  installing 115, 116
  reference 117
consumer 10
consumer groups
  managing 145, 146, 147
consumer position
  checking 171, 172
consumer statistics
  monitoring 181, 182, 183, 184
ConsumerGroupCommand tool
  about 145
  arguments 147
currency price enricher
  about 92, 94, 95
  running 96, 97, 98
currency price extractor 90, 92

D

data
  ingestion, from Kafka to Storm 203, 204
  inserting, from Kafka to SolrCloud 207
  moving, between Kafka nodes 194, 196
  pushing, from Kafka to Elastic 205
  storing, in Cassandra 213, 214
decommissioning 170
DumpLogSegments command
  arguments 148

E

Elastic
  reference 199
Elasticsearch
  installation link 205
enriched-messages 107
events
  modeling 58, 59, 60, 99, 100
extract, transform, and load (ETL) 196

F

Flume
  data, moving between Kafka nodes 194, 196
  reference 194, 196

G

Ganglia
  about 186
  monitoring capability 186, 187
Generic Security Services API (GSSAPI) 190
geolocation enricher 87, 88, 90
geolocation extractor 84, 85, 87
GetOffsetShell
  options 150
  using 149
Gobblin
  about 196
  reference 199
  used, for writing to HDFS cluster 196, 197, 198
graceful shutdown
  implementing 162, 163
Gradle

download link 63
Graphite
  connection ability 184, 185

H

high watermark (HW) 36

I

Internet of Things (IoT) 84
ISR (in-sync replicas) 24

J

Java
  installing, in Linux 13
JMX reporters, for Kafka
  reference 188
JMX tool
  parameters 151
  using 150
join 138

K

Kafka brokers, properties
  reference 56
Kafka brokers
  configuring 18, 19, 20
Kafka clients 114
Kafka Connect
  about 114
  reference 136
  using 131, 133, 134
Kafka consumer API
  reference 69
Kafka consumer
  building, with Akka 210, 211, 212, 213
Kafka core 114
Kafka Ganglia metrics reporter
  reference 188
Kafka Graphite metrics reporter
  reference 186
Kafka input plugin, for Logstash
  reference 201
Kafka mirroring
  reference 153

Kafka nodes
  data, moving between 194, 196
Kafka operations
  reference 120
  using 117, 119
Kafka output plugin, for Logstash
  reference 201
Kafka Producer API
  reference 71
Kafka producer
  building, with Akka 208
Kafka REST Proxy
  about 114
  reference 131
  using 129, 130
Kafka Schema Registry 114
Kafka Streams 114
Kafka topics
  configuring 21, 22
kafka-configs shell
  parameters 161
kafka-console-producer program
  parameters 26
Kafka-Consumer-Groups command
  arguments 172
kafka-topics shell
  parameters 159, 160
Kafka
  about 10
  cluster types 11
  installing 11, 12
  installing, in Linux 14
  messages, reading from 66, 67
  messages, writing to 69, 71
  reading, with Apache Beam 218, 219
  running 17
  running, on Mesos 214, 215, 216, 217
  Spark streams, connecting to 201, 202
  writing to 219, 220
Kerberos
  used, for implementing authentication 190, 191

L

Linux
  Java, installing in 13
  Kafka, installing in 14
  Scala, installing in 13
location temperature enricher
  about 107
  running 109, 110
log compaction 11
log partitions 10
log producer
  replaying 153
log segments
  dumping 147, 148
log settings
  configuring 32, 33
Logstash
  about 199
  data, moving from Kafka to Elastic 200, 201
  installation link 200

M

MaxMind
  reference 87
Mesos
  Kafka, running on 214, 215, 216, 217
message broker 10
message console consumer
  creating 27
message console producer
  creating 25, 26
message router 10
message topics
  modifying 160, 161
message, Avro schema 60, 61
messages
  reading, from Kafka 66, 67
  writing, to Kafka 69, 71
MirrorMaker tool
  parameters 152
  using 152
MirrorMaker, versus confluent replicator
  reference 153
miscellaneous parameters
  configuring 38, 39
multiple-node multiple-broker (MNMB) cluster
  configuring 55, 56

O

offset 10
Open Exchange Rates page
  reference 91
open weather extractor 105, 106
OpenWeatherMap page
  reference 105

P

parallelism 18
partition 10
performance
  configuring 31
ProcessingApp
  running 71, 72, 73, 75
processor topology 137
producer 10
producer statistics
  monitoring 178, 179, 180
project
  setting up 62, 63, 64, 65, 66, 101, 103, 138, 141

R

raw-messages 107
redundancy 18
ReplayLogProducer tool
  about 153
  parameters 154
replica settings
  configuring 35, 36
replication factor
  increasing 169
retention period 10

S

SASL
  reference, for authentication 191
  used, for implementing authentication 190, 191
Scala
  installing, in Linux 13
Schema Registry
  reference 129
  using 124, 125, 127
schemas
  reference 101
server statistics
  monitoring 174, 175, 176, 177
server.properties template
  reference 21
single-node multiple-broker (SNMB) cluster
  configuring 49, 50
  consumer, starting 53
  producer, starting 53
  topic, creating 52
single-node single-broker (SNSB) cluster
  configuring 42, 43, 45
  consumer, starting 48
  producer, starting 47
  topic, creating 46
single-node single-broker (SNSB)
  broker, starting 44
  ZooKeeper, starting 43
Spark programming guide
  reference 203
Spark streams
  connecting, to Kafka 201, 202
SSL
  reference, for authentication 190
  used, for implementing authentication 188, 189
state change log merger
  using 154
StateChangeLogMerger tool
  about 154
  parameters 155
Storm
  installation link 203
stream processing application
  about 137
  steps 63
stream processor 138
streaming application
  running 141, 142, 143

T

threads
  configuring 31
topics

  about 10
  adding 157, 159
  removing 157, 159
topology 137

V

validator
  coding 75, 76
  running 78, 79, 80, 81, 82

W

windowing 138

Y

yum 14

Z

Zookeeper 10
ZooKeeper offsets
  importing 148, 149
Zookeeper settings
  configuring 36, 37

Printed in Germany
by Amazon Distribution
GmbH, Leipzig